Kid CEO

Michael! —

Jennifer —

Blessings! —

Kid CEO

{ How to Keep
Your Children
from Running
Your Life }

Ed Young

WARNER
Faith®

New York   Boston   Nashville

Unless otherwise noted, all Scripture quotations are taken from *The Holy Bible*, New Living Translation, copyright © 1996. Used by permission of Tyndale House Publishers, Inc., Wheaton, Illinois 60189. All rights reserved.

Scripture quotations marked NIV are taken from the HOLY BIBLE: NEW INTERNATIONAL VERSION®. Copyright © 1973, 1978, 1984 by the International Bible Society. Used by permission of Zondervan Publishers, Grand Rapids, Michigan 49530. All rights reserved.

Scripture quotations marked NKJV are taken from the New King James Version, copyright © 1979, 1980, 1982. Used by permission of Thomas Nelson, Inc., Nashville, Tennessee 37214. All rights reserved.

Scripture quotations marked KJV are from the KING JAMES VERSION. Scripture quotations noted TLB are from *The Living Bible,* copyright © 1971. Used by permission of Tyndale House Publishers, Inc., Wheaton, Illinois 60189. All rights reserved.

Any emphases or parenthetical comments within Scripture are the author's own.

Warner Faith
Time Warner Book Group
1271 Avenue of the Americas, New York, NY 10020
Visit our website at www.twbookmark.com

Warner Faith® and the Warner Faith logo are trademarks of Time Warner Book Group Inc.

Printed in the United States of America
First Warner Books edition: September 2004
10 9 8 7 6

Library of Congress Cataloging-in-Publication Data
Young, Ed, 1961–
    Kid CEO : how to keep your children from running your life / Ed Young.
       p. cm.
    Includes bibliographical references.
    ISBN 0-446-69177-1
    1. Family—Religious life. 2. Parenting—Religious aspects—Christianity.
I. Title.
    BV4526.3.Y67 2004
    248.8'45—dc22   2004006487

*This book is dedicated to the men and women
who wake up every morning in the trenches of parenthood.
I applaud your selfless devotion and dedication to the toughest
assignment on the planet. My prayer is that the following
pages will help you discover the rewards of building both
your marriage and your family God's way.*

Acknowledgments

Many people helped me bring this project to completion. I thank my wife, Lisa, for being a constant source of knowledge, help, and encouragement. She has been my marriage partner for over twenty years and my partner in parenting for nearly seventeen years, and I could not have written this book without her. I thank my parents, Dr. Ed and Jo Beth Young, for teaching and modeling the kind of parenting I write about. I thank Cliff McNeely for helping me organize material and develop the final manuscript over the past year. I also want to acknowledge several other staff members at Fellowship Church—Andy Boyd, Laura Strickland, Preston Mitchell, Troy Page, and Rob Johnson—who assisted me with research, editing, and proofing the manuscript at various stages. And I thank the great people of Fellowship Church for allowing me as your pastor to discover these biblical parenting principles along with you over the past fourteen years.

Contents

Contents

Foreword

For years we have been living in a values vacuum in America. Our culture has become increasingly more permissive to the point that practically any kind of behavior or lifestyle is considered acceptable by at least some group. We are now reaping the results of decades of self-centered individualism: every thirty seconds there is a divorce in America. Sexually transmitted diseases are at an epidemic level. Every fourth child born in America is born to an unwed mother, and millions of other children are growing up with absentee parents.

The family is under attack from all sides. Some say the family is obsolete and irrelevant in twenty-first-century society. Others want to change the biblical and historical definitions of marriage and family. Still others want the government to play a greater role in raising children and want parents to be less responsible. These trends can be discouraging, but the family is not finished; it's just fragile and fragmented, and needs to be strengthened.

To strengthen today's families we must return to our Owner's Manual for life, the Bible. Since the creation of families was God's idea, he, not some current talk show host, is the trustworthy source for principles of family living. *Kid CEO* is based on God's timeless principles.

This is an important book for our time. My good friend Ed Young has done us all a great service by writing it. It is filled with practical wisdom on parenting that we all can benefit from. My prayer is that you will not only read this volume but also apply these principles as a parent so both you and your children will *"serve God's purpose in your generation"* (Acts 13:36).

Dr. Rick Warren
Lake Forest, California

Introduction

I'm Not Kidding!

Parenting has become a joke!

That's probably not what you expected to read at the beginning of a book on parenting. But I'm not kidding—it's the truth. It is not some flippant, broad-brushed statement just to get your attention. I'm simply communicating what I've observed over the past several decades as a speaker, author, pastor, and parent. And the sad thing is, parents, the joke's on us. Our kids are kidding us when it comes to leadership in the home. They have taken over the family, and we have let them.

That's why I've written this book. This book has emerged from a series of talks I put together on marriage and parenting. The response was so overwhelming, I was encouraged to put the series into print. I don't say that to pat myself on the back but to indicate to you the tremendous need for the tried-and-tested parenting principles in this book. In the pages to come I want to answer the burning question: how can parents take back control of the family?

The principles addressed in this book apply to all types of parents and all types of households. Whether in a nuclear family, a blended family, a single-parent family, a foster family, or any other type of guardianship, the caregivers are the parents in that household. And all parents, regardless of the makeup of their particular household, must understand and live out these parenting principles if they hope to create and maintain control in the home.

I wrote this book to call parents, whether single or married, back to the leadership role they were meant to assume in the home. I will share some of the parenting struggles my wife and I have experienced over the years, and some of the valuable lessons we have learned in bringing up our four children. More important, I will share with you what I believe to be the Source for the answers we seek in parenting and in life. I truly believe that the principles in this book, taken within their context, can change the trajectory of your family like nothing you've ever experienced.

A Special Word to Single Parents

In these introductory pages, I want to say a special word to those who are single parents. Figures from the 2000 U.S. Census reveal that 31 percent of households with children under eighteen years of age are single-parent families (an increase from 13 percent in 1970).[1] If you're doing the parenting thing alone, you have a heavy load to bear as the provider, the caregiver, and the disciplinarian in your home. My deepest admiration is reserved for those of you who find yourselves in this difficult role. As a single parent reading this book, you might begin to think, "This isn't for me. He's writing to married parents, and this really doesn't apply to my situation." Let me put your doubts to rest right now and assure you this book does apply to you as a single parent.

While it's true I will be upholding marriage as the central re-lationship in the home, your role as a single parent represents that vital relationship in your family. In other words, your family will be a reflection of your life and relationships, just as the family where both parents are present will reflect the life and relationships of the husband and wife. You are the leader. You set the agenda. You determine the course for your family. The temptation, unfortunately, in single-parent homes is for the reverse to happen. With the dizzying demands of work, family, and any remnants of a social life, it is so easy to allow your kids to take over. You may have just given up because you don't have the energy to fight the battles anymore. But let me be as clear as possible on this point: giving your kids control is not the easy way out. Whatever battles you don't fight now will turn into a full-blown war later on.

In fact, I would submit it is even more critical that single parents maintain what I will be calling a *parent-CEO household*. Without the buffer of another parent, even little issues can morph into additional stresses on the incredibly demanding schedule of a single-parent household. I truly believe, though, that you can establish order and control in your home. I know the road is not an easy one for you, but with the help of family, friends, and a church community, you can do it. You can bal-ance a career and a family. You can have a social life. You can discipline your children in love.

But the power is in your hands. You must be willing to make the hard choices now for yourself and for your children, know-ing that those choices will build a solid foundation for your family. This foundation of a parent-CEO environment will be especially important if you choose to marry again and find yourself in a blended-family situation.

So, single parent, this book *is* for you. I challenge you to keep reading to gain the knowledge you need to create a positive future for your family, to deal effectively with discipline in the home, and to establish household priorities. I will be addressing marriage throughout this book, because I have a special passion for communicating the priority of marriage as it relates to parenting. But the principles of taking back parental leadership still apply to you. And yes, even the section on increasing intimacy in marriage is for you, because the odds are great that you will marry again.

PART ONE

The Family Power Struggle

Who's in Charge Here?

{ 1 }

The Kid-CEO Household

MY WIFE, LISA, was approaching the security checkpoint at a tiny northwestern airport when her cell phone rang. It was a call from home. She was waiting to depart for Dallas after a weeklong trip she and I had taken together. Our oldest daughter, LeeBeth, was on the other end of the line, and not having seen us for several days, she was eager to share the latest events of her week.

As the conversation came to an end, she asked her mom's permission to attend an upcoming birthday dinner with a friend. They had discussed the details of her friend's birthday several weeks earlier, so this wasn't anything new. When she reminded my wife of the date, Lisa quickly realized why they had previously tabled this discussion. Our daughter had made a prior commitment we felt she should honor. Lisa gave LeeBeth the bad news that she couldn't go to the party that night. Her response was something less than agreeable.

She quickly began to counter with all the reasons why she

just *had* to go to this dinner on this particular night. She explained to her mom this was the only night her friend could have the dinner, and it would ruin everything if she couldn't go. This was the same song, second verse, she had sung the last time they had this conversation. But after hearing her out for several minutes, Lisa stood her ground and told her that the prior commitment stood. LeeBeth was told that if it was that important for her to be at the dinner, she would have to see if her friend could rearrange her plans.

Once again, our daughter did not take her cue to accept defeat graciously and respond appropriately. Instead, her exact words in response to my wife's final decision on the matter were: "Mom, you've got to be kidding me!" Somewhat taken aback by her challenge, my wife responded, "LeeBeth, when it comes to parenting, I don't joke around!" That was the end of the conversation.

"When it comes to parenting, I don't joke around!" I wrote in the introduction that parenting has become a joke, but make no mistake: parenting is serious business. And we are going to get down to some serious business in the pages to come. A power struggle is brewing in the home that is no laughing matter—a family power struggle that we, as parents, need to identify and win.

A Nationwide Power Struggle

Just like the tension my wife experienced on that phone call from our teenage daughter, some major tension is being expressed in families everywhere as a result of an ongoing power struggle in the home. Lisa and I won the power struggle with our daughter, but many other parents are losing ground.

Homes that look great on the outside, with beautiful architecture, white picket fences, and immaculate lawns, on the inside are packed with confusion, conflict, and chaos. Parents, let's face it: there is a crisis buried deep within the family. Families are out of control. This crisis has been brewing right under our noses, and sadly, the majority of us have yet to smell the coffee.

What is happening in these homes is a crisis of leadership. The truth of the matter is that leaders aren't leading. Parents in many families today aren't stepping up and paving a path of purpose. In fact, what is happening is a role reversal. In other words, kids are running the asylum. They are leading, and the parents are following. As a result, the home has become a lopsided landslide of mayhem—it has become kid driven rather than parent driven.

The wild thing about this misguided ideology is that popular culture actually applauds and supports this lopsided household. Hollywood actors parade themselves on talk shows and talk about how their kids are little kings and queens in their homes. But don't be fooled, because this is not an applause-worthy state of affairs. In homes of the famous and not so famous alike, parents and their kids are engaged in a pivotal power struggle for control of the family.

This tug of war begins the moment the ob-gyn slaps a baby on the rear end and says, "It's a boy" or "It's a girl." Immediately, an organizational shift occurs. With the entrance of a child into the family system, a dual resignation takes place. The wife resigns from her primary role, that of being the wife, and she becomes a mother. She immerses herself in the lives of her children, their every need, want, and desire. In essence, she marries them. If she is one of the three out of five mothers who also work outside the

home,[1] the additional demands of her career pull her even farther away from the marriage.

Likewise, the husband resigns from his primary role, that of
being a husband, and becomes a father. With the additional responsibility of children, he also begins to step up his role, usually
as a career chaser. Oftentimes, the desire to succeed and become
the financial provider for the family becomes the driving force of
his life. He buries himself in his work, putting the demands of
the job before everything else. In essence, he marries his career.

Meanwhile, the marriage relationship gets pushed farther
down the line of priorities. Marital drift takes place, and eventually a giant chasm forms between the husband and the wife,
leaving the marriage open and vulnerable. Given the right (or
wrong) set of circumstances—an attractive coworker, the
NASCAR pace of family life—and . . . you get the picture!

Who Reports to Whom?

With the marriage no longer the focal point of the home, the
child becomes the center of their universe as the parents orbit
their marriage, their interests, and their schedule around the
life of their little one. Over time, they relinquish more and
more control to the child. The child gets a taste of power and
likes it. He begins to get comfortable in the family study, sitting in the high-back leather chair and propping his feet up on
the mahogany desk. And make no mistake, this seemingly innocent child will do anything to protect his position of power.

In this backward model, the parents report to the child, and
the marriage connection takes second place to what has become the family's primary focus: the kid. Extracurricular activities and professional responsibilities rob the marriage of

quality time, regular intimacy, meaningful conversation, and emotional connection. With both spouses chasing the kids and one or both chasing a career, the calendar chaos sabotages the marriage. These distractions create a seemingly insurmountable distance that can't be bridged unless something drastic takes place to fix the family system.

Similarly, in a single-parent household, the demands of career and kids pull simultaneously to keep the parent from having meaningful adult relationships, from scheduling social activities, and from generally having any pursuits other than those the kids dictate. Given the limited resources, time, and energy of a single parent, the children's ability to gain power in the home intensifies. And unfortunately, this overwhelmed and overworked parent is often too tired to fight for the authority that is rightly his or hers to claim.

Basically, these scenarios typify what I will refer to throughout this book as the *kid-CEO household.* Sadly, this particular power structure has come to represent the norm in the American family today. Edward VIII, Duke of Windsor, once observed this about American families: "The thing that impresses me most about America is the way *parents obey* their children" (emphasis mine). Within that veiled humor is a startling truth. We are witnessing in many homes today the devastating effects of a family system gone terribly wrong. From moral confusion to failing marriages, from the decay of discipline to organization frustration, out-of-order homes are producing out-of-order children.

The kid-CEO household didn't just show up overnight. A decades-long history has led up to where we are today. After World War II and the onset of the baby-boom generation, many well-meaning parents turned their backs on conventional wisdom and started following permissive parenting persuaders, Dr. Spock among them.

In order to be completely clear on this point, let me define what I mean by the word *permissive*. I defer to the definition offered by noted psychologist and author Dr. James Dobson: permissiveness is "the absence of effective parental authority, resulting in the lack of boundaries for the child. This word represents childish disrespect, defiance, and the general confusion that occurs in the absence of adult leadership."[2]

Permissive parenting sounded good at first. It was a fresh, new approach to parenting that promised a more liberated family environment. In essence, this parenting style encouraged parents to crawl into the crib with the child and reason with their rebellious toddler. Permissive parenting touted a democratic and egalitarian household, but in reality it was all about giving the child undivided attention and constant nurturing. Rather than bringing equality, it robbed the parents of authority and elevated the child above everyone and everything in the household.

Permissive parenting is not just a thing of the past. It is still alive and well today—perhaps even in your own household. And while it may not sound so bad on the surface, there is a major problem with it. The problem is that permissive parenting doesn't work. Children are not designed to lead the family. They are not hardwired to call the shots or to handle that level of responsibility, because they do not have the maturity or the skill set to do so. Yet parent after parent resigns his or her leadership position, hands in the keys to the family study, and turns over the decision-making power to the child: "Where do *you* want to eat?" "What do *you* want to do tonight?" "When do *you* want to go to bed?" "Where do *you* want to go on vacation?" "How may I serve *you*?" In short, they create a kid-CEO home. The kid-CEO household, however, is the opposite of God's dynamic design for the family.

God's Dynamic Design for the Family

While standing on the banks of the Buffalo River in Moran, Wyoming, I was awestruck by the order and organization evident in creation. From the waterways flowing from the heart of the Grand Tetons to the fish and wildlife that get their food and water from their life-giving supply, I realized with greater clarity at that moment that everything has a certain order, flow, or system to it. Successful companies are well organized. Winning teams work together in perfect harmony. And dynamic families must also function according to their design in order to go and flow as a unit.

The great thing about the design for the family is that there is no need to wonder what that is or where to find it. Because God is a God of order, he has already established an organizational pattern for all of creation, including the family. This may be a foreign concept to you. You may never have seen a statement like that before and wonder where I got such an idea. In the introduction of this book, I wrote that I believe there is a Source for the answers we seek in parenting and in life. That Source is God himself. He has written the book on life and in that book, the Bible, we can find the answers for what is unarguably life's most challenging role, that of parenting.

Throughout the coming pages, I am going to quote various passages from the Bible that relate to parenting. If you have a Bible handy and want to look these up yourself, that's great, but I will always include the actual wording from each passage as well as where you can find it in the Bible. Even if these biblical concepts are a bit new for you, I ask you to keep reading as we take a closer look at God's dynamic design for the family.

The Family Flow Chart

First of all, picture in your mind a flow chart. Do you know the kind I'm talking about? Businesses use these to determine the chain of command in a company. The head of the company is at the top—the CEO, the president, the executive director, or whatever title has been designated for that office. We are going to use a similar flow chart to map out the chain of command in the family. In the top box of the family flow chart, we are going to write a single three-letter word: *God*.

$$\boxed{\text{GOD}}$$

God is at the top of the organizational chart for everything, including the family.

The Bible, life's instruction book, tells us, "Follow God's example in everything you do, because you are his dear children" (Eph. 5:1). We're God's children. Isn't that an incredible thought? If we have established a relationship with God through his Son, Jesus Christ, we are children of God. And as his children, we are to imitate him in word, thought, and action. That means that we should obey him. It's that simple. His standards should set the standards for how we behave as parents and how we teach our children to behave.

You could say that God is the first order of order in the home. For Christ-followers, that should be a given. The first two of the Ten Commandments—"Do not worship any other gods besides me" and "Do not make idols of any kind" (Exod. 20:3–4)—place

God at the center of our existence. So naturally it follows that he should be at the center of our homes as well. Service in the community, love for our neighbors, good manners, a strong work ethic, effective discipline, a thriving marriage—all of these flow from this first order of order in the home.

The next tier of the family flow chart relates to the marriage relationship. Again in Ephesians 5, we see God's design is for man and woman to unite together in the spiritual and physical union of marriage (5:21). The significance of this relationship is made clear by its comparison to Christ's relationship with the Church (5:25). It is a picture of Christ's sacrificial love for us. And it is built on mutual love and respect flowing from that supernatural love. God is first. And then the love relationship between husband and wife comes second.

After our love for God, there is no greater love than that of a man for his wife or a woman for her husband. What that will look like on our flow chart is this: in the same box we will write *Husband* and *Wife* and draw a horizontal line connecting the two words. It looks something like this:

The two are side by side and in the same box to signify that they are one flesh and coequal in the eyes of God. The Bible teaches that marriage, the one-flesh connection between man and woman, is the most important human relationship in the family. This special union between husband and wife was originated by God in the very beginning (Gen. 2:24) and continues to be the foundation of both family and society.

A successful family begins by putting God first and then working to make sure the marriage relationship takes a place of prominence in the family. The best thing you can do as a parent is to have an amazing marriage. It is the greatest gift you could ever give your children. As the marriage takes its proper place, everything else in the family will fall in line. I cannot say this enough: as the marriage goes, so goes the family.

You may wonder as you continue to read this book, "Is this book about parenting or marriage?" It is about both. I do not believe you can talk about reclaiming parental control of the home without addressing the priority of marriage. Even if you are a single parent, you must understand the critical importance of the marriage relationship in the family dynamics before you even consider entering into another marriage.

Can you see the family flow chart beginning to take shape? God is at the top. The husband and wife are in the next tier. And then below them are the children. On our chart, there will be a line coming from the *Husband—Wife* box to a box below them labeled *Children*.

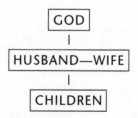

Later in the book of Ephesians, we read, "Children, obey your parents because you belong to the Lord, for this is the right thing to do" (6:1). Children fall in line under the parents' authority. This has been God's design from the beginning.

You may be thinking, "Ed, are you saying that children are not important? Are you saying that we should not love them sacrificially?" No, that is not what I'm trying to communicate. I love my kids, and I would give my life for them. But the relationship I have with Lisa, my wife, must take priority over my kids, just as my relationship with God must take priority over my wife.

If that sounds harsh, it's not. Setting these priorities is the most loving thing you and I can do. When we follow God's organizational plan, the rest takes care of itself. Our love for God serves as the motivation to love our spouses as Christ loved the church, and then that Christlike love we have for our spouses serves as a model of love for our children.

Have you begun to identify a leadership crisis in your family? If so, you may need to initiate a leadership takeover of your home. If your children are taking top tier on the family organizational chart, it's time for you to tell them to clean out their office. You're not firing the children, but you're moving them to the position they should hold. That's what this book is all about. I am going to show you how you can take your proper role in the home as parents and how to put your kids in their place as well. Remember, God has an order for everything. God is not a God of chaos; he's a God of organization. There is a flow chart for the family, a chain of command. And we must follow that chain of command if we hope to have a family that is running on all cylinders.

Parenting Defined

Before we go any further, I need to establish a working definition of parenting. I believe, for many reading this book, the definition of parenting I am going to introduce will be a little shocking. But I must clarify up front that this is not my definition; it is God's. We have already established that as husbands and wives, we must defer to God's chain of command in the home. So, if we're going to understand what it means to be a parent in God's family flow chart, we must also understand and download his definition of parenting.

Here is the definition of parenting: *parenting is the process of teaching and training your children to leave.* That's right. The goal of biblical parenting is to prepare children to leave the home. "Wow, Ed," you might be thinking, "that's pretty harsh stuff. Do you not like your kids, or something?" Yes, I love my kids, but I also understand my role in their development is to prepare them for life—to get them ready to leave our home and start homes of their own. Believe it or not, I didn't just pull this stuff out of the sky. The Bible clearly states that this is what should happen: "A man leaves his father and mother and is joined to his wife, and the two are united into one" (Gen. 2:24).

This means children should individuate; they should become autonomous from their own parents. They should hook up with spouses, and marriage should then become the primary human relationship as all the other relationships become secondary. The long and short of parenting is that we are to teach and train our kids to leave the home, cleave (or join) with their spouses, and weave families of their own.

We will dig deeper into this definition later in the book, but let's look briefly at the two main elements of parenting. The teaching element is found in Deuteronomy 6:6–7: "And you must commit yourselves wholeheartedly to these commands I am giving you today. Repeat them again and again to your children. Talk about them when you are at home and when you are away on a journey, when you are lying down and when you are getting up again." As parents, we are to make an intentional and strategic effort every day to teach our children God's principles, so they can go out into the world and establish their own households built on solid and eternal values.

The training part is represented in Proverbs 22:6: "Train a child in the way he should go, / and when he is old he will not turn from it" (NIV). Notice the word "go" in this passage. It does not say "stay," does it? Too many families have children living at home who have overstayed their welcome. We have in this country an epidemic of twenty- and thirty-something adults who are in a state of prolonged adolescence and still living at home, because their parents have not embraced this parenting principle. These adult children like the comforts of the corner office and executive perks too much to give them up. They are pulling in a nice salary and enjoy the benefits of free room and board. Mom does the cooking, the cleaning, and the laundry. That's a pretty sweet deal. But if we are doing our jobs as parents, this is the exact scenario we should be trying to avoid. If you follow God's flow chart, you should be training your children by way of example to leave and establish homes of their own.

As you look at the flow chart for your family, it should read: *God, Husband—Wife, Children.* If it doesn't read that way, what are the first steps you need to take to reorganize your family? The answer is not an easy one. In fact, some of the concepts to follow may even sound harsh at first. But I assure you these steps are in the best interest of your kids. I am outlining them in the first chapter by way of introduction, but you will find expanded elements of these throughout the book.

Reorganize

If you are in a kid-CEO household, the first thing you need to do is reorganize. God has put certain people over you for a reason. He put certain people over me for a reason. The same is true with this flow chart. Parents think they need to give their children undivided attention 24/7. But we need to realize it is possible to give our kids too much attention.

Kids need oxygen, but too much oxygen will smother them. Kids need attention—there's no question we need to spend time with them regularly and strategically—but too much of a good thing can suffocate them. It can be counterproductive to the overall goal of parenting. Too much attention gives them the idea that they are in the driver's seat and Mom and Dad are just passengers on the bus.

In his book *Good to Great,* Jim Collins presented the results of a study of companies that have moved from mediocre to meteoric. One of the things he found was that great companies not only get the right people on the corporate bus, so to speak, but also get the right people in the right seats on the bus.[3] The problem with many families is that while the right people are on the family bus, they are in the wrong seats. In the family bus, parents should sit in the driver's seat. If there is a void in the driver's seat, kids will quickly fill it and do everything they can to stay in it. Family counselor and author Gary Smalley wrote about a child's propensity to make a family power play: "A child senses that he is in the driver's seat and can play the parent accordingly."[4] You don't have to teach kids how to do this. They know how to gain control of the seat of power and then take their parents for a ride.

Again, it's not going to be an easy thing to put your kids in their proper seat on the family bus. They like the driver's seat. They like setting the course. They like the power that comes with controlling the accelerator and revving up the family engine. And believe me, they're not going to give all that up very easily. However, if you do not take back the key to the bus now, it will end up hydroplaning over what you need to be and do as a family. The longer you let them sit in that high-backed driver's seat, the harder it will be to retake control.

Set the Agenda

This reorganization process takes place as you begin to change your behavior and set the agenda for your family. You do this not only by what you say but also through your own example. You must model the priorities you dictate to your children. Parents set the schedule. Parents step up. Parents cast the vision. Parents move ahead. They don't get everybody's opinion and then make a democratic decision. The permissive parenting style teaches that all members of the family carry equal weight in terms of authority and decision-making. But everyone is not equal in the family. Spiritually before God we are equal, but in terms of the practical organization of the family, there is a flow chart and a prescribed chain of command. God has placed parents over children for a reason. Parents, we must lead and set the agenda for the family.

Before I highlight some specific issues related to this, let me be clear again why you need to take such a firm line of authority as a parent. You need to communicate to your children (maybe even in a family meeting) that you are doing what is best for the entire family, and that begins with keeping your marriage a priority in the home. As I address several different practical issues in the next few sections, I will show you how it benefits both your children and your marriage. Marital issues cannot be compartmentalized into a neat, tidy little chapter. They are part and parcel of everything you do as a parent, so I want to communicate to you how the marriage is benefited and impacted throughout this process of setting the agenda in the home.

Say Good Night!

We will be looking at many different practical issues related to setting the family agenda throughout the book, but by way of illustration in this opening chapter, let's start with a perennial problem area in every household. Let's look at the dreaded issue of bedtime. I believe establishing a bedtime routine is one of the bedrocks for household organization and structure. Most parents agree, at least in theory, that bedtime is very important. Taking that theory, though, and living it out on a daily basis is where most of us fail. Too often we allow our kids to decide when they want to go to bed. But deep down, children really crave a structured routine set by their parents.

Small children, especially, need to have a regular bedtime. By establishing a pattern early in their lives, you are establishing a pattern for all of childhood. The actual bedtimes may change, but the principle of a parent-CEO bedtime should remain the same.

Many kids today are sleepwalking through life because parents are not enforcing this fundamental routine in their family. An April 2003 article entitled *Experts Say Kids Need More Sleep* reported the findings of the National Center on Sleep

Disorders Research regarding children and sleep. These experts say, "Families just aren't paying enough attention to the importance of sleep." They go on to say, "A tired child is an accident waiting to happen." If your children are regularly exhibiting "crankiness, lack of focus or difficulty controlling emotions," you probably need to make a change to the bedtime routine. The article gives the following advice to parents: "Schedule a 'quiet time' each evening, and keep distractions such as TV, games and computers out of kids' rooms." Sleep experts recommend a minimum of nine hours of sleep for kids, and the only way for that to happen in most households is for kids to go to bed earlier.[5]

Lisa and I have four kids. We have a teenager who is sixteen, an eleven-year-old son, and twin daughters who are eight. During the school year, our eleven-year-old and our eight-year-olds go to bed around 7:45 to 8:15. That's their bedtime, no debate, no questions asked. Lisa and I set this time by figuring out how much time it takes us to connect once the kids are asleep. That has worked well for us. It has done great things for our marriage and great things for our family.

Now, with our teenager, it's a little different. When the clock hits nine, she knows to disappear to her room. She can stay up for a while, talk on the phone to her friends, listen to music, do some homework, or whatever she wants, but she has to stay in her room. Now, we don't let her stay up all night. She understands that within an hour or so free time is over and she needs to be in bed.

Take Time to Connect Daily

An established bedtime is good for your kids, and it is also good for you. Parents, do not ask your kids, "Are you sleepy?

Are you ready for bed?" Instead, put them down when you are ready, based on the agenda you have set. You are not putting them to bed early just for their benefit; you are doing it for the benefit of your marriage relationship, which in turn benefits the whole family.

Our children know that Mom and Dad need time to connect. By word and example, we are communicating to our kids that what we have going on as husband and wife is very important. I need to emphasize, though, that just because we have the time to connect after the kids have gone to bed does not mean that it automatically happens. Many temptations encroach upon those few precious moments Lisa and I have together in the evening. Some of those temptations come from the technological distractions that fill our lives and our homes. Gary Chapman also noted the sense of isolation that technology can bring: "Some sociologists feel that advanced technology has encouraged individuality and isolation, that we have turned our efforts toward becoming a success as an individual, and that we have lost the concept of succeeding as a family."[6] Don't let technological temptations ruin your family time or the limited time you have with your spouse.

One of the toughest temptations is the urge to pick up the remote and channel surf for the rest of the evening. I'm not saying you or I would ever do this, but I've heard some people fall asleep in their easy chairs with the remote controls embedded in their hands. Let me say this as simply as I can: put down the remote, and spend some time with your spouse. Here is a challenge I like to give to married couples: don't just turn off the television and put down the remote; unplug the television and take it out of the bedroom. A television should not be in the bedroom. The same goes for the computer. Instead of channel surfing, you may be tempted to surf the Web late into the evening. Take the computer out of the bedroom, and if the Internet is coming between you and your spouse, cancel your Internet service. The bedroom should be a place of intimacy, a place of joy, and a place of conversation.

Perhaps your temptation is the telephone. Instead of picking up the remote, you pick up the phone and have two-hour phone conversations with a friend or relative. Lisa and I often have phone-free nights on which we agree not to answer the phone or make any outgoing calls. If you are one of those people who can't stand to let a phone ring without picking it up, then turn off the ringer. It really is okay to let the phone ring without answering it. Say this to yourself every night: "I am the master of the telephone. The telephone is not the master of me."

Here's another temptation: do not let housework or office work distract you from spending quality time alone with your spouse. If you need to complete some work, then agree together to set a time limit. Spend an hour on work and the rest of the evening talking together in front of the fire, going for a long walk, reading a book together, holding hands on the patio and watching the stars (or the mosquitoes if you live in Texas), or, dare I say, making passionate love together. Take time to connect in a real and intimate way after your kids are in bed, and you won't believe where it will lead.

Limit the ECAs

The next thing parents must do to take back the leadership role and to set the agenda is to place a reasonable limit on your children's ECAs. I'm referring to extracurricular activities. I know that you as a parent want the best for your children, as do I. But the question begs to be asked: what is the best? Most of the time, the answer to that question involves limitations, discipline, and sacrificing the good things for the great things.

If you asked parents, "What is the best thing you could give your child?" most would answer, "A strong moral and spiritual foundation to carry them through life." In theory we believe that, but in practice many of us allow other things to distract us from that ultimate goal. Oftentimes, those other things are all of the extracurricular activities that fill our afternoons, evenings, and weekends. Many parents have allowed ECAs to take priority in their families: cheerleading, dance or voice classes, basketball, football, baseball, hockey—you name it. All of these activities are jockeying for our time and our kids' time, often pushing out the things that matter most.

Extracurricular activities help kids, and I am definitely not advocating a ban on ECAs. The lessons and skills they can learn in these activities and experiences are good. But these merely good things have a way of eclipsing the great things. Oftentimes, ECAs are in direct conflict with marital and family times where those moral, spiritual, and intimate foundations are formed.

When children reach the age of twelve or thirteen and face difficult choices, when they're trying to negotiate the maze of life, what are they going to rely on? On cheerleading or football or basketball? Those activities are not going to give them the knowledge and wisdom to help them make those tough choices. They need a sure foundation. And the ultimate foundation is found only in a growing relationship with God. Don't let culture decide what is important. You make that decision as parents who know what's best for your kids.

We're in a fight—a fight for our families and our marriages.

And one of the major weapons in our arsenal is how we use our time. Too many families are overscheduled and over-whelmed with merely good stuff, while they are missing out on all of the great things God wants for them! The key to scheduling extracurricular activities for your kids is proactively establishing priorities. It is beneficial to have kids in school and community activities, but these must fall in behind church activities and the family's spiritual growth. When these merely good things begin to encroach upon your spiritual de-velopment, take a long, hard look at the ECAs. Parents, it's time to step up and limit the ECAs for our children.

Date Your Mate

The final, and perhaps most important, idea I want to intro-duce in this first chapter about setting the agenda is the need to date your mate. Yes, that means actually going out on dates the way you did before you were married. I believe so strongly in this marriage principle that by the end of the book, you will probably get tired of reading about it. But please do not miss the importance of these regular one-on-one times in building a marriage that will outlast the parenting years.

Let me also emphasize here that this section on dating your mate is just scraping the tip of the intimacy iceberg. I have in-cluded an entire section on marital intimacy during the par-enting years, but I want to highlight the importance of this principle now as a foundational priority in reorganizing the home.

Here are several reasons why you should date your mate. The first is that it makes economic sense. It pays huge divi-dends to date your mate. I know what you're thinking: "Ed, what does dating my spouse have to do with economics?" The long-term payoff of regular dating is the money you will save on divorce lawyers later on! If you don't keep romance and intimacy as top priorities, if you neglect the marital date night, divorce will come knocking at your door. So, why not date the man or woman who stole your heart years ago? It will save you a lot of money and heartache in the long run. Noted author and psychologist Henry Cloud wrote, "A marriage is only as strong as what it costs to protect it."[7] Pay the price now to keep your marriage on solid ground.

The second reason you should date your mate is that it makes spiritual sense. Marriage is a holy covenant. In fact, marriage is a spiritual commitment on steroids. You are modeling to others around you what it means to have a great marriage. You have made a covenant before God to love, honor, and cherish this person for life. Fulfilling that covenant is a mark of spiritual growth and maturity. The marriage relationship is so important that it represents the relationship Christ has with the church. It is a spiritual and mystical union that gives us a human picture of the spiritual and mystical union of the body of Christ. When you are making a regular, intimate connection with your spouse, your relationship with God will be impacted in a positive way.

It makes economic sense and spiritual sense. And third, it also makes relational sense. By going out on dates and leaving your children with a sitter, you are modeling what marriage should be for your kids when they grow up. Dr. Laura Smith reminded us of the importance of modeling as parents: "If you want your kids to turn out well, you need to demonstrate the values, behavior, and self-control you want to see in them."[8] Dating your mate teaches your kids that Mom and Dad's marriage is the most important relationship in the family. It also teaches them independence and responsibility. They learn early on that sometimes Mom and Dad will leave together, but they also learn that they will come back.

If you are worried about their crying when you leave, think about the alternative. You can either let them cry for a few minutes now, or you can cry a river of tears later when your marriage ends up on the rocks because you didn't make the date night a priority. The choice is up to you. Kids are going to cry, and most of the time it's good for them. Don't let a few tears keep you and your mate from doing what you know is most important for your marriage and your family.

Let me ask you again: how does your family fall in line with God's organizational chart? Maybe it's time to take a long, hard look at who is sitting in the study—in the corner office. Whose rear is parked in the driver's seat of the family bus? Who's running the show? Who's sitting in the corner office? If you have allowed your kids to take over the family, you need to make the choice now before God to reorder and reorganize your family. As a godly parent, commit yourself right now to being the kind of leader God meant for you to be, to do this family thing God's way. The last time I checked, God's way is the only way for true success—in marriage, in the family, and in life.

This commitment is the most important step in creating a parent-CEO household. As you get into the rugged plains of reality, you will be tempted to turn back. Your kids will not welcome the change (in fact, they will fight it tooth and nail), and especially in the initial stages it would be so easy just to give in to them. So set your resolve to stick with this program for the long haul. And then, having made that resolve, keep reading to discover the details of what a parent-CEO household looks like.

{ 2 }

The Parent-CEO Household

I WAS SITTING IN a local coffee shop early one morning, minding my own business, studying and doing some research on marriage and family issues. Just a few feet away, a toddler-toting mom was sitting in a comfortable chair talking to another woman. While sipping their morning brew, these two women engaged in deep dialogue.

I was sitting right next to these women, but I could tell they were oblivious to me. When the conversation turned to parenting, I naturally could not help but listen in. The toddler-toting mom was talking about the challenges of child rearing and how to maintain a good marriage with her husband's busy travel schedule. The other woman, between sips of coffee, was discussing whether she and her husband were even mature enough to have kids.

Finally I decided I had heard enough and just had to butt in; I said, "Excuse me, ladies." They turned and looked at me as if they were thinking, "Oh! Someone else is here?" I said, "Do you mind if I ask you a couple of questions? I'm doing some research on marriage and parenting." They agreed, and as I began to probe a little into their particular situations, they opened up and shared some of their concerns about marriage and family. After a while, it was time for me to head to the office, so I packed up my briefcase and headed toward the door.

As I was leaving, the toddler-toting mom turned, looked at me, and made a statement that I will not soon forget. She said, "You know, I think I'm a great mom, but not that great of a wife."

As I thought about that statement, it occurred to me that a lot of parents today would echo that same frustration. I think many would say, "You know, my kids are getting a lot of attention. But my spouse and I aren't really connecting anymore."

There are some important underlying questions within this woman's statement. She is admitting that her life is out of balance. There is a flaw in the flow chart. By expressing the frustration that she is a better parent than spouse, she is asking several critical questions: "Should my home be a kid-CEO home? Should the children control all of the activities and all of the scheduling? Or should my family be a parent-CEO unit where the parents run the show and where the marriage has the ultimate priority? Which one do I put first: my marriage or my kids?" We are going to find the answers to those questions in the next few pages.

In the first chapter we established that in many households, the kids are running the family show. The kids are sitting in the office, calling all the shots. We also said that we need, as parents, to be parents. That involves, among other things, reorganizing our homes and reestablishing parental authority in them. Being a leader means speaking the truth in love—we do what's right for our children, not what always makes them feel good.

And as leaders, we also need to cast the vision for our family. What that involves, first of all, is making the marriage the most important priority in this earthly thing called "the family." Therefore, the primary focus of what I call the parent-CEO household is keeping the marriage relationship strong and vibrant during the parenting years.

The current cultural norm is to place kids in the nucleus of the family cell. And unfortunately, Christian families more often than not conform to this norm rather than set the trend. What we must understand, as I hope to show you in this chapter, is that the parent-CEO household makes sense from a practical perspective, a relational perspective, a logical perspective, and most important, a moral perspective. If we want to grow strong families, the marriage must remain in the nucleus of the family cell. Everything else in the family system revolves around and is driven by this key relationship.

Dr. John Rosemond was one of the pioneers in recognizing the need to refocus the family on the marriage relationship. In his book *John Rosemond's Six-Point Plan for Raising Happy, Healthy Children,* he said very pointedly, "For those of you who are married, the secret to raising happy, healthy children is to give more attention to the marriage than you give to the children."[1] In other words, the marriage should be the center, or the nucleus, of the family.

If you know anything about science and biology, you know the nucleus is the brain of the cell. It contains the stuff of life, the power that gives a cell the ability to function properly and to relate to other cells. The same is true in the parent-CEO household. Mom and Dad, your one-flesh relationship is the powerhouse and the center of life for your family. When you lose this focus, your family cell will begin to atrophy.

For the family unit to function properly, our goal as parents should be truly to hold the place of leadership in our homes. We must understand our role as parents and teach our children their proper role as kids.

In order to illustrate what the parent-CEO household is all about, I have to show you first what it does not look like. And to do this I want to introduce you to several types of parents that I have affectionately labeled the Alphabet-Soup Parents.

Alphabet-Soup Parents

Do you remember eating alphabet soup? As a kid, I used to really go through that stuff—you know, "Mm, mm, good." The great thing about alphabet soup was that I could eat and play at the same time, two of my favorite things to do. I dipped my spoon in that piping hot alphabet soup and then used my fingers to arrange the noodles on the spoon to spell certain words. I'm sure you have similar memories of playing with your alphabet soup.

One of the problems we have in parenting today, moms, dads, and single parents, is that we have a bunch of Alphabet-Soup Parents running around. Alphabet-Soup Parents have rearranged the letters in the family soupspoon and have created jumbled-up parenting styles that don't work. Scores of well-meaning parents arrange the letters to conform to cultural expectations rather than to what God expects for the family. I don't say that to be mean or harsh, because many, many parents are simply unaware of how to do it God's way. They are parenting the way they think it should be done or perhaps the way their parents modeled it to them. Or they may just be re-acting without any preset agenda to whatever crisis, problem, or challenge comes along. This chapter, and this book, is aimed at breaking these dysfunctional parenting styles by learning what God's agenda is for the home and then deciding ahead of time as parents to follow that agenda.

The EMT Parent

The first set of Alphabet-Soup Parents is the EMT Parents. With the speed and efficiency of an emergency medical tech-nician, these parents are experts at rescuing their kids from every problem, scrape, and conflict. Rather than encouraging independence in their kids, these parents foster a chronic de-pendence through their constant rescuing behavior. Furthermore, personal responsibility has no meaning for the children brought up by EMT Parents. Nothing is ever their fault. It's always the teacher's fault, the coach's fault, another child's fault, or even another parent's fault. These parents are great at playing the blame game because they cannot accept the possibility that their own child is at fault for anything.

Well, how does EMT Parenting play out over time? The most likely scenario in these households is that the overindul-gent, overprotective, and overcommitted EMT Parents end up handing over the family study in the home to their kids. In her article "The Perils of the Pushover Parent," Carol Lynn Mithers cited the current epidemic of kids who have been handed con-trol of everything in the home: "Many kids today take for granted that they govern family activities and decisions. The concept of not getting what they want, when and how they want it, is wholly unfamiliar to them."[2] As the household con-tinues to orbit around them, they become spoiled, sassy, and rebellious children. And eventually, they turn into spoiled, sassy, and rebellious adults. So go the lives of EMT Parents and their children.

The NCAA Parent

Let's turn to another set of Alphabet-Soup Parents that is common in today's competitive culture: the NCAA Parents. These are moms and dads who see their kids, from the time they can crawl, as stars in the making—super athletes, brilliant doctors, high-powered attorneys, or world-famous actors. These parents tend to be overly demanding, living out their unfulfilled dreams through their kids and pushing them to succeed at all costs. They are committed to and engaged with their children, but they are also highly directive and harsh in their discipline and expectations.

This type of parent sees him- or herself as a coach or trainer and the child as a recruit. You know the kind I'm talking about— those "I'm going to push my children to be exceptional even if it kills me"-type parents. You might hear them saying things like this to their kids: "Hey, give me forty push-ups. If you don't hit at least forty push-ups a day, you're not going to make it into the NBA" or "You'll never be a doctor with those grades" or "You need to shape up or you won't get accepted into Harvard Law." There's nothing wrong with encouraging our kids to excel, but these parents are over the top. Running the home like drill sergeants, they are hard, unrelenting, and rigid.

The YMCA Parent

Another common category of Alphabet-Soup Parents is the YMCA Parent. If you remember, the YMCA is the organization that invented the "buddy system." That's the system designed for places like swimming pools, so that when the lifeguard blows his whistle, everybody holds up the hand of his or her buddy and yells, "Buddy! Buddy!" The lifeguard can see that everyone is swimming with his or her buddy, friend, or pal, and that all are present and accounted for in the pool.

YMCA Parents are those who are into the buddy system with their kids. They place their children's little hands in their big adult hands and yell, "Buddy! Here's my buddy, my friend, my pal." But I've got a news flash for parents who are playing house according to this system: it is not our goal as parents to be our kids' best friends. Unfortunately, I see this all the time in parent-child relationships: "I just want to be a buddy to my child. You know, I just want to be one of the gang." While this tendency is certainly understandable, it has damaging ramifications for parental authority in the home.

Please don't misunderstand me. I'm all for camaraderie and having a good time with our children. We need to play with them, take part in regular recreational activities with them, and spend quantity and quality time with them. Those things are a great and essential part of parenting. However, we must never lose sight of the fact that we are, first and foremost, the parents. We are the leaders in the home, and it is our job to shape the lives of our children, not to hold their hands and be their buddies. Yes, a part of our relationship can be categorized as friendship, but we must not stop with friendship. Friendship is not the goal of parenting. Parenting, as we will see throughout the coming pages, has a much broader and grander agenda.

The Ph.D. Parent

The final parental style common today is that of the Ph.D. Parent. These parents are the overthinkers. They try to reason with their kids, to compromise and psychoanalyze. They treat their kids like little adults, expecting them to be able to make informed choices before they are ready. And these parents also tend to push their kids academically to succeed, oftentimes putting student achievement at the forefront of the family agenda.

In their attempts at reasoning and psychoanalysis, they tend to morph into permissive parents. They are engaged in that Dr. Spock mentality we addressed in the first chapter—the mentality that says that everyone is equal and the home is sort of a microdemocracy. Children, though, have a keen ability to use this parenting style to their own advantage. While Ph.D. Parents want their children to see this egalitarian approach as an opportunity for democratic debate and consensus, kids growing up in this type of household see it as an opportunity to manipulate the system and get what they want.

Am I saying that democracy in society doesn't work? No. I am saying that democracy in the home doesn't work. Children do not yet have the knowledge and perspective to decide what is best for them. Children tend to live in a little universe called Me, and their decisions are usually based on their immediate wants and needs. It is our job as parents to help them, over time, to see the bigger picture and understand the world around them. But until then we need to decide what is best for our kids, simply because we are the grown-ups and we know better.

Setting Some Expectations

What's the basic problem with all of the parenting styles I just mentioned? To put it plainly, they don't work, and they do not honor God. But if you want a "wheels off" family, if you want your kids running the show, and if you want to have a messed-up marriage, then by all means choose one of the Alphabet-Soup styles of parenting. On the other hand, if you want a family that moves in perfect sync, if you want kids who respect your leadership, and if you want a dynamic and growing marriage, you need to choose God's way. And God's way is the parent-CEO household.

Before we get into the details of what a parent-CEO household looks like, I need to warn you about the ramifications of making the decision to take the leadership role back in your home. When you decide to trade places with your kids and do what you should do as parents, what's going to happen? What can you expect? Your kids may have been in charge for a while. They are comfortable in the driver's seat; they like being at the controls. You, on the other hand, may be a little uncomfortable with that position. You may not even remember how to turn on the ignition or adjust the driver's seat. So, naturally, with this change in leadership you can expect a little tension to occur.

Here are some things to keep in mind as you make this transition from a kid-CEO family to a parent-CEO family:

- *Keep your eye on God's agenda.* Don't lose sight of God's flow chart for the family and the ultimate rewards of doing the family thing his way.

- *Recommit to the marital relationship.* It's going to take complete unity between husband and wife to make this happen. Before you make the move to reclaim leadership in the home, make sure you are committed 100 percent to keeping your marriage a priority. The growth of

that relationship should be the benchmark of family
success.

- *Expect conflict.* The power struggle is likely to get worse
  before it gets better. If your kids are used to running
  things, they are not going to give in without a fight. But
  remember, as a parent, you're the leader. You have the
  authority and the responsibility before God to restore
  order in your home.

When your kids begin to get a little rebellious about this
whole idea of a parent-CEO household and try to talk back to
you, I encourage you to do something I call the *Parent Rap.* I
made up this rap several years ago, and it's something your
kids just might need to hear:

> *I'm the parent. I'm legit.*
> *There's no use arguing; you might as well quit.*
> *You can roll your eyes and say it's not fair.*
> *But you're just telling God you really don't care.*
> *So do what I say all of the time,*
> *then your life will have serious rhyme.*
> *All the time, yours and mine, peace of family mind.*

Do you want to have peace of family mind? Then remember
the *Parent Rap,* and even when the going gets tough, don't give
up on being large and in charge in your home.

How to Reestablish Parental Leadership

So far in this chapter we have looked at several parenting styles
that don't work. These common styles all have one thing in

common: they lead inevitably to a kid-CEO household. We have also established that something needs to change, and that is for parents to step up and take back control of their homes by establishing a parent-CEO household. In addition, I have set forth several expectations that parents need to keep at the forefront of their minds as this transition takes place.

With all of that as a backdrop, we are now going to turn to what needs to be done in practical terms to reestablish parental leadership in the home. The remainder of this chapter will set the stage for the rest of the book in terms of what a parent-CEO household looks like and how to achieve it.

Cast the Family Vision

First of all, we must as parents and leaders cast the family vision. And for Christian parents, that vision must come from only one place: God. God tells us in Proverbs 26:12, "Where there is no vision, the people perish" (KJV). As the pastor of a large congregation, I have discovered people forget the vision of Fellowship Church about eight weeks after I've given a message on it. That's why we say it, we spray it, we wheel it, and we deal it as often as we can. Fellowship Church exists to reach up—meaning to worship, expressing love to God. We also exist to reach out—meaning connecting Christ with others. And we exist to reach in—meaning discipleship, having Christ fully formed in our lives. That is the mission of Fellowship Church, and we try to communicate it in as many ways as possible. As parent leaders, you should have a vision, a mission statement, for your family, and you should communicate that vision as often as possible to your kids.

At this point you may be thinking, "Well, I guess I had better go out and try to formulate a vision for my family. I wonder what the vision should be." You don't have to worry about that. You can just relax, because the vision is already spelled out for you. Joshua, in the Old Testament book by the same name, gave us the vision for our families: "As for me and my household, we will serve the LORD" (24:15 NIV). That's pretty simple, isn't it? Joshua didn't take a vote. He didn't consult *Robert's Rules of Order*. He didn't put together a focus group, a think tank, or a committee. What did he do? He stood up as the leader of the household and said, "As for me and my house . . ." And basically that's the first part of the *Parent Rap*: "I'm the parent. I'm legit. There's no use arguing; you might as well quit." That's what he said in a loose paraphrase. "I'm the chairman. This is what we're going to do. We're going to follow the Lord. We're going to seek him as a family."

Sadly, we have allowed the culture to dictate our vision. We are bombarded with messages from society about what our priorities should be. Some say, "Education is the key." Others say, "No, government holds the answer." Still others cry out, "Technology rules the world; put your hope in technology." Financial success, athletic achievement . . . the list goes on and on. All of those things have places in our lives, but they don't deserve first place.

Go against the grain, and follow God's vision for your family. We have already looked at God's flow chart for the family. His priorities for our homes are simple and strategic: God first, marriage second, and then the children. Follow Joshua's lead and cast the vision. And then keep it at the forefront of your minds and hearts as a family. Say it and spray it, wheel it and deal it every chance you get. Have it engraved and put it in a prominent place in your home: "As for me and my household, we will serve the LORD."

Build the Vision

After you cast the vision, you need to take the next important step: build the vision. Vision is great, but you have to strap it to commitment, endurance, and some specific objectives in order to carry it through. I know many parents who talk about vision all day and night, but they have never done the stuff to make that vision a reality in their homes.

Using Fellowship Church again as an example, we have staff retreats every year. Our leadership team goes off somewhere, and we talk about the vision of the church. But we don't just stop at talking about the vision. We spend the majority of our time building the vision, which involves setting specific goals and objectives in order to fulfill our mission. And if we ever begin to discuss objectives that don't fulfill the mission statement, we throw them out.

K.I.D.S.

God has goals for you and your family, and he mentions those goals throughout the Bible. The rest of this book is going to develop four objectives for your marriage and family that will help you realize the vision of a parent-CEO household. These objectives are built around the acrostic KIDS. We have already established the family unit is not to be kid driven, but I want you to remember KIDS when you think about your family's goals and objectives. This acrostic will be a reminder not to let your kids run your home, but to do family the parent-CEO way.

By way of introduction, let me briefly outline each of these four objectives in this chapter. And then each succeeding section of the book will address specific ways these are played out in the home.

*K*nowledge That's Grounded

The *K* in KIDS stands for *Knowledge that's grounded.* We have to have a knowledge that's grounded in the Bible. That incredible book has the answers for our families, and as parents we are responsible to lead, teach, and train according to that knowledge base.

Entire books have been written that make a case for the validity and relevance of the Bible in our lives today, so I won't try to do that in a paragraph. Let me just say this: you may not read the Bible on a regular basis, but you can be assured that the principles and precepts within its ancient pages have withstood the test of time. Through thousands of years of debates, research, questioning, and challenges in the fields of science, theology, and philosophy, the Bible remains the most-read, most-bought, and most-sought-after book of all time. I find it amusing that most self-help books today borrow from biblical principles but present these principles as if they were something new.

Mom and Dad, as you soak in the wisdom available to you from the Bible, you are building a reservoir of knowledge that your kids need. The problem is that it's being dammed up because you aren't exercising your authority in your home. It's time to turn that reservoir of knowledge into a river of knowledge. Being a parent leader is all about making good choices. And parents have the knowledge base, the experience, and the wisdom they need to make hard choices for their kids.

We must understand, as the grown-ups in the house, that just because a kid wants something does not mean it will be the best for him or her. Parents are there to make the best and wisest choices for their kids. And in the process, they help their kids get to a place over time where they can make wise choices for themselves.

It should not be a matter of debate whether or not we know more than our kids do. You may think otherwise when you're trying to help them with their algebra homework, but for the most part, we have greater experience and knowledge than our kids. And because we know more than our kids know, it is our job to help them negotiate the maze of life.

*I*ntimacy That's Intentional

The *I* stands for *Intimacy that's intentional.* Do you realize the more children you have, the less intimacy you are likely to have as husband and wife? I talk to couples regularly about this subject, and they tell me, "Oh, we wish we had more intimacy. We wish we could spend more one-on-one time together." Just in case you aren't catching my drift: I am talking about romance and sex. Most of us as parents aren't romancing our mates, dating our mates, or having regular, meaningful times of physical intimacy with our mates.

We have to fight for physical intimacy. We have to fight for the date night. And we will explore specific ways to do that later in the book. But let me just say this right now: parents, it's worth the fight to keep the love, the romance, and the intimacy alive in your marriage during the parenting years. I'll say it again: the best thing you can do for your kids is to have a great marriage. If you don't, your kids will never launch from your home with great trajectory. As parents, we have to spend time connecting—relationally, sexually, and emotionally. That's the superglue of marriage—that coming together regularly as one flesh and celebrating God's great gift of the marriage bed.

Discipline That's Consistent

The *D* in KIDS represents *Discipline that's consistent.* It should come as no surprise to you that we're going to have to discipline our children. Parenting is not a popularity contest. It's not the YMCA buddy system or the Ph.D. roundtable discussion. Consistent discipline is one of the earmarks of a parent-CEO household. And believe it or not, kids cry out for discipline.

Watch your children, at whatever ages they are, and observe ways in which they test the boundaries you've set up. If the boundaries aren't there, though, they will move closer and closer to the edge until one day, they fall off. Kids crave the protection of parental boundaries, so the parent-CEO household should be characterized by loving and consistent discipline. Too many parents are capricious, rather than consistent, with their discipline. Discipline should be consistently enforced with a unified front between Mom and Dad, so the kids always know where the boundaries are and where both Mom and Dad stand.

We discipline those we love for their protection and growth. The great leader in society is a man or woman who is disciplined. Likewise, a great leader in the home is not afraid of confrontation or discipline because he or she always does it with one goal in mind, which is to teach and train children in the ways of the Lord. Drs. Henry Cloud and John Townsend used the following illustration to highlight the importance of consistent discipline and strong parental leadership in the home: "You are like an oak tree that the child runs her head into over and over again, until she realizes that the tree is stronger than she is, and she walks around it next time."[3]

God uses a strong arm of discipline in our lives because he loves us and wants to keep us from making painful mistakes. Discipline in God's economy is simply correction driven by love. Our heavenly Father disciplines us to teach us, and as earthly parents we are to use consistent and strong discipline in our kids' lives for the same reason.

*S*tructure That's Strategic

Finally, the *S* in KIDS stands for *Structure that's strategic*. A lot of families are so uncontrolled, so off-the-wall, that kids are screaming for structure. They're crying, "I want it! I want it!" So parents give it to them! Gary Smalley said this about a child's need for structure and the long-range benefit of setting boundaries in the home: "Study after study has demonstrated that children need boundaries in order to grow up with a healthy sense of stability and security. By providing that for them, we give them one of the greatest gifts any parent can give a child."[4]

The parent-CEO household is not a military academy, but it is a home based on structure and routine. If you feel like you have a wheels-off family, characterized by chaos instead of order, it is time to make a strategic effort to create the family flow chart, set the expectations, establish the routine for your family, and then stick to it. You won't believe what will happen when your family members move together in organizational unity. It's an incredible thing. But it starts with the parent.

A structured home is really all about priorities. Jesus said in Matthew 6:33, "He will give you all you need from day to day if you live for him and make the Kingdom of God your primary concern." When we make the things of God our primary concern, everything else falls into place. It's all about giving him first priority in our homes.

I love the word *priorities* because the word *prior* is in it. See, we need to set our priorities prior to the activity. A lot of us aren't living priority-driven lives, and you can't have a parent-CEO home that is not priority driven.

Instead of setting our priorities prior to our activities, we are letting the "ities" get us. What are the "ities"? It's when the activ-"ities" of the day drive us instead of our letting our priorities drive our activ-"ities." All day long we go from this "ity" to that "ity," here an "ity," there an "ity," everywhere an "ity," "ity." The "ities" attack us when we make decisions about our priorities only after the activity hits. Don't do that. Make those crucial organizational and prioritizing decisions prior to the "ity"!

Before the activity, you ask: "What are our priorities as a family?" Then you ask: "Does the activity we are considering encroach upon our relationship with the church? Does it encroach upon our marriage? Does it encroach upon what's most important for our children?" Set your priorities prior to the "ities," and you'll be way, way ahead of the game.

Do you know what priorities are? Priorities are simply saying yes to the best. That's what it means to have great priorities. God wants the best for you, but to say yes to the best, you sometimes have to say no to the good. Nowhere is that principle more critical than in the marriage relationship. Drs. Cloud and Townsend said it nicely: "A life of 'yes' to everything else ultimately results in a 'no' to your marriage."[5] We've got to learn how to say no to some things, and we'll learn more about how to do that in chapter 8.

*   *   *

Knowledge. Intimacy. Discipline. Structure. These are what the parent-CEO household are all about. It sounds very practical and very simple, doesn't it? But it takes courage, Mom and Dad, to make this happen in your family. And it takes work. We will discover, however, in the following pages that doing the hard stuff now to make your family run the way God intended will save you from a lot of even harder stuff later on. The family power struggle is yours to win, if you will dig in your heels and accept nothing less than victory. As you learn how to experience victory in these four areas in the pages to come, you will see the parent-CEO household is the only way to go. Do it for your marriage, and do it for your kids.

PART TWO

Knowledge

Building the Family Foundation

{ **3** }

Strengthening Foundations
for Fragile Times

THE RESEARCH AND STATISTICAL DATA from the past few decades regarding the family looks pretty grim. In fact, I'm not trying to depress you, but it looks bad on most fronts. From the divorce rate to the number of single-parent households, from couples living out of wedlock to domestic violence, and from teenage pregnancy to sexual abuse statistics, the numbers become outdated the moment the ink dries on the page.

While it may appear that the family is lost in a morass of immorality, there is a positive side. Change is possible if we want it bad enough. We are ingenious enough to preserve humpback whales, bald eagles, and snail darters, so I think we are ingenious enough to preserve the future of the family, don't you? I believe many, many people in America understand there's a problem and want to work toward a more positive future for the family. In fact, recent polls show that 80 percent of Americans believe immorality is the number one issue in our country and want to make a change.[1]

The problem, however, is that while we don't lack the desire to make a positive change, we sometimes lack the knowledge we need. That is why, over the next few pages, I want to focus on gaining the know-how necessary to build both a strong foundation and a positive future for our families. It is our job as parents to think about and plan for the future, but as Dr. Henry Cloud pointed out, "We tend to parent in the present without thinking about the future."[2] We are taking the lead from our children, who have a natural inclination to live in a present-tense world. Instead, as parents, we must begin to build a solid foundation for our families by looking toward the future.

The knowledge we need for this forward-looking approach has one purpose: to accomplish the goal of parenting we addressed earlier in the book. Again, that goal is to teach and train our children to leave the home and establish lives of their own. With that objective in mind, I want to give you six principles you must download into the hard drive of your parent-CEO household. These principles can help forge a positive outlook as you begin to trust God with the future of your family.

Six Principles for a Positive Future

1. Pass on *Faith*

The first—and most important—way to establish a positive future for your family is to pass on the baton of faith. Parenting is a relay race. Those who want to win the race are good at handing off to the next generation the essentials they need to live a life of faith. But here's the catch, parents: we cannot pass anything to our children that we do not possess ourselves. Many families live in constant chaos because they don't have the power of faith operating in their homes. We can tap into that power if we get serious about having a relationship with God and living lives consistent with his truth. When we do that, we pass on the baton of faith to our children on a daily, moment-by-moment basis.

How do we go about passing this kind of faith on to our children? Again, we must turn to the Bible. Let's look once more at the words of Deuteronomy 6, which, as we have already seen, are a biblical cornerstone for the parent-CEO household. These eternal words talk about the daily discipline of faith building in the home: "And you must think constantly about these commandments I am giving you today. You must teach them to your children and talk about them when you are at home or out for a walk; at bedtime and the first thing in the morning" (vv. 6–7 TLB). The commandments Moses referred to in this verse are God's commandments—those transcendent principles of love, honor, obedience, integrity, kindness, and faithfulness that are true for all people, in all cultures, at all times.

What does it mean to teach these transcendent principles to your children? It is very important that we understand the meaning of the word *teach* in this key parenting passage of the Bible. The Old Testament Hebrews had two definitions for *teach*. The first was the idea of a formal lecture, as in a professor giving a lecture in a classroom on parenting, child rearing, or the family system. Our idea of teaching in the Western world is very similar to this concept of a formal, organized presentation.

However, that is not the meaning of the word *teach* in this passage. The other meaning had to do with the casual, every-day conversation of life, and that is the meaning the writer used here. He wanted to get across the idea that character training flows more out of a parent's day-to-day encounters with his or her children than it does from formal teaching. Whether you talk about baseball or ballet, music or math, the color of the sky at dusk or the dew on the grass in the morning, every conversation can provide an opportunity to teach your children about the things of God. I like what Kurt Bruner, a vice president with Focus on the Family, said about this process: "We must become intentional about teaching our children the values we consider important. It is not a matter of when we will have the time, but rather a question of if we will take the time to make a plan."[3]

The basic meaning behind the term *teach* is that parenting never stops. You are always—*always*—teaching your kids something. There are no downtimes, time-outs, or do-overs. Everything you do, every moment of the day, teaches your children something about life, whether you are in their presence or not. The time you spend away from them at your job, at social functions, on dates with your spouse, on the golf green, or on business trips speaks to them about the importance of each of those activities. You pass the baton of faith moment by moment, in a thousand seemingly insignificant words, phrases, activities, and conversations. In other words, just as in a relay race, the baton is not taught, it is caught "when you are at home or out for a walk; at bedtime and the first thing in the morning."

Christianity is not just a weekend sport. It is a Monday, Tuesday, Wednesday, Thursday, Friday, Saturday, and Sunday lifestyle. Those teachable moments with our children can happen while they are playing Xbox or PS2, while they are at the soccer field, shopping at the mall, playing at the piano recital, fishing, or camping. And when your children give you those windows of opportunity, take them, parents, and teach them words of faith.

When I think about what it means to pass on the baton of faith through teachable moments, my mind rushes back to when my son EJ was four years old. EJ, at that age, was the quintessential picky eater. His diet consisted primarily of cheese crackers and Frosted Flakes, and trying to feed him anything of a healthier nature resulted in an almost daily power struggle. Well, one night Lisa and I were determined he was going to eat grilled chicken. We placed four little bites on his Spiderman plate, but he immediately began to cry that he didn't want it. So we said firmly, "EJ, we are going to sit here until you eat the chicken." Finally, he stabbed a piece of chicken and slowly lifted the fork to his mouth. If you have, or have had, a four-year-old, you know what's coming. Just as it touched his tongue, he gagged dramatically.

Many sincere Christian parents try the same thing we did with EJ when it comes to matters of faith. They try to force religion down their kids' throats. They take a hose, open up their mouths, and force, force, force. This is not how we are to teach the things of God. Rather, teaching happens as we live our lives. I thank my parents for passing the baton of faith. They didn't force it. They didn't say, "We are going to sit here until you take it, Ed." They lived out authentic Christianity in front of me, and as a result, I caught the baton by choice in God's good time.

I'm not criticizing formal teaching. On the contrary, I grew up hearing about character and virtue and the things of God, but those ideas and words became real to me because I saw them acted out through my parents and other adults.

Allow me to sum up this point by recapping the three primary ways in which you can pass the baton of faith to your kids.

First, adopt the teachable-moment methodology. When those opportune moments come up in the midst of your daily life, give your kids words of faith at the age-appropriate level. So many parents miss out on this critical area because they think they have to lecture their children to teach them anything. Lisa Beamer, wife of 9/11 hero Todd Beamer, wrote this about the daily business of teaching values to our children: "It's not necessary to lecture or sermonize, but by interacting with your children on a daily basis, stay alert for opportunities to illustrate the difference between worldly values and godly ones."[4] Take advantage of every teachable moment that comes your way to instill transcendent values into your kids.

Second, do not force-feed faith to your kids. You cannot make your children adopt your faith. In fact, the more you try, the more you will push them away. The greatest spiritual asset you can pass on to your children is that of living out an authentic faith in front of them. If you are trying to indoctrinate your kids with religious ritual but aren't expressing your faith in a real and consistent way, you are missing the boat entirely. Your kids don't need meaningless ritual; they need a faith that works. And the sobering reality is that if you aren't modeling to your kids an authentic faith in Jesus Christ, you may be opening the door for someone else to model to them a faith contrary to that. Good parenting is all about letting your life become a living lecture for your children to see and emulate.

Third, take advantage of the church to assist you in this process.
I venture to guess you have an incredible local church somewhere near you. The church is the last, best hope for the future
of our families and our society. You cannot pass on the baton
of faith if you aren't actively involved in a church where your
kids receive age-appropriate teaching. Get them involved in
preschool, children's church, youth group, or whatever programs your church has. The number one complaint of the
workers who staff the children and youth areas in my church
is the inconsistent attendance among families. If your children
aren't there on a regular basis, it's virtually impossible for the
church workers to teach them and develop meaningful men-
toring relationships with them. Their spiritual development
within the church becomes a hit-and-miss proposition.

It is vital, Mom and Dad, that you utilize and support the
resources of the church to help build faith in your children.
What do you want most for your kids? If your answer is that
you want them to grow up to be people of outstanding character and faith, then the church should hold a central place in
your family's schedule.

2. Build Your Home with *Understanding*

We also have to develop a proper understanding of how our
family of origin affects our present-day family and how that in
turn affects our children's future families. The Bible tells us,
"By wisdom a house is built, and through understanding it is
established" (Prov. 24:3 NIV). Our parents built the beginning
of that foundation early on in life in the construction yard of
our childhood homes.

Sometimes it's a scary thing to say something to our children
and then immediately realize, "That sounded exactly like my

mother. I can't believe I said that." Or to look in the mirror one day and realize that you are turning into your father. I had this happen to me several years ago while I was in a clothing store to purchase a suit. I asked if I might try it on to make sure it fit. I proceeded into the dressing room and changed into it. As I stood in front of the full-length mirror, in a moment of self-realization I thought, "I'm turning into my father! My hair is getting gray, and my dad has two suits exactly like this! What am I doing?"

The really scary part of growing up to be just like our parents is the fact that our children will do the same thing as they grow up. They will eventually walk, talk, dress, and look like we do. And they will also, most likely, grow up to be the kind of parents we were to them. We tend to parent the way we were parented. We tend to resolve conflict the way we saw conflict resolved. We tend to have an honesty quotient like our parents' honesty quotient. Do you see how important it is, parents, to model authenticity and integrity to your children? If you don't understand the importance of the foundation you are building for the generations that follow, then you have every reason to be fearful for your children's future.

On the other hand, if we continually make the right choices as parents, we don't have to fear for our families. I have written an entire book on the subject of fear, entitled *Know Fear,* in which I outline ways that we can face the many terrors that loom large in this world. The premise of the book is that oftentimes we are fearful because we choose to be. The fears we face are in large part due to the poor choices we make throughout life. If we make bad choices, we face bad consequences and all the fears that go along with them. If we make good choices, we face a brighter future and better consequences.

Admittedly, it's not always that clear-cut. Many, many

things are out of our control. But we can eliminate a multitude of our fears by making the best possible choices regarding those things over which we do have some control. And then, having done what we know to be right, we trust God to take care of the rest. This is especially true when it comes to making choices that provide the best possible foundation for our children to have a bright future.

3. Prepare for Family *Transitions*

The family is in a constant state of change, so as wise parents we prepare for the future by anticipating and planning for family transitions. The biblical king and philosopher Solomon said everything is appropriate in its own time, but we cannot see "the whole scope of God's work from beginning to end" (Eccl. 3:11). We cannot possibly know all that will transpire over the years within our families—only God knows that—but there is a time of transition we can see on the horizon and must be ready to negotiate.

Children are born in what some psychologists call a "one-down relationship" with their parents.[5] This means that authority-wise they're on a level one step below that of the parents. Then, as parents give them more and more decision-making rope, they move from a one-down relationship to an eye-to-eye relationship. Then, ultimately, they leave home. Five times the Bible repeats that a man should leave his parents and become one with his wife. Parents, when our children are young, we direct them. When they get older, we coach them. When they become adults, we consult with them when they ask for advice.

Jesus never married, but even he went through this experience of pulling away from his parents. Mary and Joseph, his parents, were going home one day and suddenly realized Jesus wasn't with them. I'm sure it looked like a scene out of the movie *Home Alone*: "Where is he? I thought *you* had him!" They went back to the temple to look for him and found Jesus, at twelve years of age, debating the religious leaders on issues of faith. They asked, "Jesus, where have you been?" He said, "Don't you know, Mom and Dad, I have to be doing my Father's business? I have to carve my own course. I have to forge my own future. I have to determine my own destiny." He recognized, and so then did Mary and Joseph, the transitional stage of child rearing.

Parenting is all about transitioning our kids from childhood to adulthood. But too often we avoid the difficult realization that our babies are growing up. Instead of giving them more decision-making rope, we turn the rope into a leash and pull harder. Part of building a positive future means preparing ourselves for this transitional phase and being sensitive to our children's own awareness when it's time for the parent-child relationship to change.

4. Recognize Your Children's *Uniqueness*

Parents who understand the goal of parenting also recognize their children's uniqueness. These parents encourage and support the unique personalities, gifts, and character qualities that will propel their children through life. This individuality is one of the trademarks of the human creation.

God made each one of us completely unique, from our DNA to our fingerprints, from voice quality to eye color, and from talents to behaviors. When our twin girls were twenty months old I began to observe a fascinating difference in behavior between them. Oftentimes Laurie walked up to the television set and turned it on and off, on and off, on and off. I'd say, "Laurie, no!" And Laurie, being sensitive to the word *no,* would back up and not do it again. Conversely, when Landra walked up to the television set and turned it on and off, on and off, on and off, and I said, "Landra, honey, no!" the behavior continued, on and off, on and off, on and off. "Landra, no!" On and off, on and off, on and off. If I took a step toward her, she backed up. But if I turned around again, she went right back to the same old game.

How can this be? Twins, brought into the world by the same people, living in the same home, the same culture, the same environment, and the same context are completely unique individuals. For years, child development experts embraced the "lump of clay" theory: children are all alike, and parents can form them any way they choose. Now, the experts have taken a 180-degree turn and are basically saying, "Sorry, we messed up. Each child really is different and unique from birth."

Of course, as usual, social science is confirming what we have known all along. Incidentally, isn't it about time we used a little common sense when it comes to listening to the advice of so-called experts? At the risk of quoting an expert to warn against the advice of experts, we would do well to heed the words of Dr. John Rosemond in this regard. "Raising children," he said, "is not fundamentally difficult, but the 'experts' make it sound difficult, and we have made the mistake of believing them."[6]

Wise parents don't need the help of experts to see their children are unique. They recognize the natural bents of their kids and work accordingly with them to train them up within the context of their God-given abilities and talents. (The final chapter will provide a greater discussion of training children according to their individual gifts and talents.) The difficult part of appreciating uniqueness in our kids is when, for instance, you have a Type-A-personality father—a hard-driving, goal-oriented person—with a Type-B son who is into the arts. How do you affirm the uniqueness of your son when you are wired totally differently from the way he is? I think God has a purpose in giving us children who are completely unlike their parents. You might think he does that because he has a sense of humor (and perhaps that's true), but I believe it's mostly intended to stretch us and teach us how to recognize our kids' uniqueness.

As you applaud your child's individuality, keep this truth in the frontal lobe of your mind: "I am fearfully and wonderfully made" (Ps. 139:14 NIV). That word "fearfully" relates the idea that the human creation is an *awesome* wonder. As you recognize the fear and awe with which God created your children, you are acknowledging your fear and awe of the Creator himself. Being a parent who fears the Lord means training your children according to the unique way God made them and recognizing the individual worth their Creator has given them.

5. Model *Respect*

If we want to provide a positive future for our children, we should also model respect. The Bible says, "Don't make your children angry by the way you treat them" (Eph. 6:4a). The idea here is that parents should not put unrealistic and unreasonable demands on their children. Instead it says, "Bring them up with the discipline and instruction approved by the Lord" (v. 4b). This means loving discipline. We are to model our parenting after our perfect heavenly Parent. God does discipline us as his children to improve us, but always out of love and respect.

Late one evening I was in the grocery store buying a few items, and I stepped into the fifteen-items-or-less express lane with my purchases. The lady in front of me had about thirty-seven items, so I had a little time to kill. I glanced over at the supermarket tabloids lining the magazine racks, and one of the cover stories caught my eye. It was about some secret vacation photos of a famous celebrity couple. I reached over, opened the paper, and looked at the pictures. I thought, "That poor family. They can't go anywhere without the paparazzi following them." It showed this famous guy with his hair plastered all over his face after a big wave hit him unexpectedly. His equally famous wife was shown removing sand and grit from her children's ears.

Seeing those candid photos reminded me about what it's like being a parent. Parents, we have little paparazzi following us wherever we go. Little eyes and little ears are taking photographs and recording conversations. Everything we do and don't do, everything we say and don't say, every core value that we give to them—they are taking it all in. What are your children seeing in your life, in the way you parent and discipline them? Are you making them angry by giving unrealistic and inconsistent demands? Or are you communicating respect by lovingly correcting your children with the goal of improvement in mind?

6. Know Your Kids' *Environment*

The final principle is that we need to know the influence of the environment in which our kids spend the bulk of their time. I love to fish, and I talk about it all the time. When I get a chance to go saltwater fishing, my favorite fish to catch in the world is the silver king, known as the tarpon. I read about tarpon constantly, specifically about their environment. We don't live near salt water, but I know more than most people would probably ever care to know about the tarpon's environment. I know what tides they like. I personally tie the kind of flies they eat. I am a student of the tarpon, because I know I can't catch them if I don't know their environment.

As a parent in today's culture, I have to ask a brutally honest question: do you really know the environment and the influence your family is under right now? Do you know what's out there? Jesus warned us to "be as shrewd as snakes and as innocent as doves" (Matt. 10:16 NIV). Are you being shrewd parents?

In John 17:15 Jesus prayed to his heavenly Father regarding his followers, "I'm not asking you to take them out of the world, but to keep them safe from the evil one." Our children live *in* the world, but they should not be *of* the world. So we need to pray, as Christ did, that God will protect them from evil and help us provide a foundation that nurtures, not hinders, their spiritual development.

It's all about focusing on the family mission I have been articulating all along. Ricky Byrdsong, in his article "Coaching Your Kids in the Game of Life," wrote, "There are times when as parents we need to call a halt to business as usual, we need to intervene in the way our kids are going . . . so that we can focus on the mission."[7] That's proactive leadership in the parent-CEO household. It's our job to intervene in whatever way necessary to make sure the proper foundation gets built. The wrong kind of foundation can debilitate us and keep us from moving ahead in life. The right kind of foundation, on the other hand, can motivate and propel us forward toward all that God wants for us, as parents, and all that God wants for our children.

Finally, did you catch the little acrostic in the six principles I just talked about? The first letter of each keyword—*F*aith, *U*nderstanding, *T*ransitions, *U*niqueness, *R*espect, and *E*nvironment—spell out the word *future*. That was no happy accident. I did it that way because I truly believe if we apply these six principles, our families can have a positive future built on a firm foundation.

{ 4 }

Under the Influence

EVERYTHING CHANGES when you have kids."

I've heard that sentiment expressed often, but every day the reality of it hits home in a hundred different ways. Everything feels different, looks different, sounds different, and tastes different. After the entrance of children into our home, I began to look at the world through a new set of lenses. I especially began to evaluate the influences of our culture on the minds and hearts of my children. The music, the arts, the movies, the TV shows, the Internet, the schools, and the government—all of these societal entities took on a new and profoundly different reality as they related to my family.

Just recently I was shocked into awareness of how, despite my best efforts, the worst aspects of our culture have infiltrated the protection of the home. My family fell prey to a tragic statistic related to the Internet and children. One afternoon, while doing a search on the Internet for a homework assignment, one of our nine-year-old twins came across an image that adults, let alone someone her age, should not see. Linked deceptively to a Web site that appeared to be something else was a graphic image of a couple engaged in a sex act.

As you can imagine, my wife and I were incensed and horrified that our daughter accidentally saw something like this. But as you will find out later in this chapter, this is not an unusual occurrence. Children are being exposed to images like this at younger and younger ages, due in large part to the proliferation of the Internet into our lives. Because of what happened in our home, in addition to having already installed filtering software (which obviously can't catch everything), my wife and I have had to completely restrict our three younger children from all Internet access unless we are present. You may think that's too radical, but I don't. We have to take radical steps to protect our children from the insidious material that threatens their hearts, minds, and souls.

Daydreaming of the Ideal

As I reflect on the harmful cultural influences that have found their way into the home, I often wish things could be different. I wish we could experience what we often refer to as a "heaven on earth." Jesus said, in what is now referred to as the Lord's Prayer, "Your will be done on earth as it is in heaven." And I wonder what it would look like if we indeed could experience God's will on earth, or heaven on earth.

In an effort to help satisfy my curiosity, I did an informal survey by asking several people this question: "If you could create the perfect environment here on earth, what would that include?" Here are some of their more humorous responses; perhaps they sound like some things you'd like to see in this world of ours. In an ideal world:

- You would set the taxes, and the politicians would have to pay them.

- You would birdie every hole.

- You could eat all the chocolate you wanted and never suffer the consequences.

- Food that is good for you would taste good, and food that is bad for you would taste bad. In other words, bagels would taste like Twinkies and oat bran cereal would taste like Froot Loops.

- Exercise would be pain free.

- There would be no receding hairlines.

- There would be no computer freezes.

- Credit cards would pay you interest.

- Your cell-phone batteries would last forever.

- You would never have a bad-hair day.

- Sun exposure would be good for your skin.

- Every fish you caught would be a ten-pound bass. (This was mine.)

Obviously, I listed the more humorous wishes. Many more-substantial wishes were also mentioned, like no more war or sickness, no hunger or pain, and everyone would have a friend. And all of those things would be nice. But since this is a book about the family, I have to ask: What would heaven on earth look like in the family unit? What would the perfect family look and act like? Do you ever wonder that?

Here are a few of my ideas. First of all, in a perfect world the family would teach, model, and reinforce the transcendent values God has given to us. I am referring to transcendent values we discussed in the previous chapter such as love, commitment, honor, and obedience. The mom and dad in this family, because of their love for God, would love each other passionately, treasure each other, and be committed to each other to the grave. This mom and dad would also love, honor, and cherish their children.

In a similar manner, their kids would respect and obey their parents. They would not fight with each other, would do their homework and chores when asked, and would grow up to be fine, upstanding young people because of their upbringing in this utopian household. That would be a great family, wouldn't it?

Unfortunately, most families don't look like this. Why is that? What keeps families from achieving this kind of home environment? Educators and politicians alike stand behind lecterns and on the backs of tractors giving lip service to the idea that "we have to get back to family values." And we need to get back to family values, they say, because the family that really teaches values can stand up against anything. It is strong. It is resilient. It is like the classic Timex watch ad: families can "take a licking and keep on ticking."

Do you believe that? Do you believe the family can take anything? Is that true or false? I hope you said false, because the family cannot take on the whole world by itself and emerge unscathed. We need a little help to make this family thing work the way it's supposed to.

The family was never intended to be the only entity to teach and model and inspire and live out transcendent values. God intended it to be a team approach. No doubt about it, the Bible says categorically and unequivocally that the family is to be the launching pad of these values, but other elements of society have to hold up their end of the deal for it to really work. The question is: are they doing it?

Heaven on Earth

If music and the arts, Hollywood, the media, the government, and school systems were to join the family in teaching and upholding transcendent family values, that would be the closest we could come to heaven on earth. Let's daydream about that for a moment. I want you to join me on a quick stroll through what this hypothetical spiritual utopia for the family would look like.

To begin with, when this perfect family breaks after breakfast, the kids rush off to school. The school system in this world is phenomenal, because it's run by men and women who reinforce the values the family teaches and models and inspires. Teachers in this incredible school do not assign meaningless homework or an amount that takes away valuable family time in the evenings. The curriculum is historically and scientifically accurate and does not present unproved theories as fact. Extracurricular activities in these schools do not interfere with the family or church activities. And in the classrooms, teachers do not leave morality up to polling data but make their classes cooperative training grounds that teach respect for authority and traditional principles.

As you would envision, Mom and Dad give each other high fives because the school is right behind them. These educational systems are doing their job in this spiritual utopia.

After seeing their kids off to school with confidence the teachers will support the values they teach at home, Mom and Dad head off to work. And believe it or not, the people who own the companies and who wield the power on the boards base their decisions on how each will affect the family. They compensate generously. They have substantial medical benefits. They give fair job descriptions. They allow for adequate vacations so working parents can spend lots of quality time with their families. And the workdays always end in time for employees to get home, greet their kids after school, and prepare a delicious and nutritious meal for the whole family to enjoy together. We are talking about a perfect work environment, so let's throw one more in just for fun. In this utopian workplace, employers encourage parents to work out of their homes, if possible, in order to cut down on the commute that eats away valuable family time.

The government is also on target in this utopian world. A society built around family values has to have solid leadership, so the government officials in this heaven on earth also make decisions that highlight and reinforce the transcendent values the family teaches. Along with the support of the schools and the workplace, this government really does things that help the family. Its taxes are not overbearing. It provides safe neighborhoods. Its laws are moral and just and based on God's principles. It recognizes the tremendous challenge facing families and does not financially support anything with tax dollars in the arts or business that would undermine the family. The leadership in this government is truly something to behold.

What about the media? As you would expect, the media moguls are on top of it when it comes to supporting the family. The television producers and movie executives produce creative documentaries, made-for-television movies, dramas, and sitcoms that again lift up those transcendent values the family unit is teaching. They avoid vulgar language, sexual situations, and gratuitous violence. Instead, they present stories that teach character values such as honesty, hard work, excellence, courage, fairness, generosity, faithfulness, love, patience, and kindness. The media in this perfect world works hard to present positive and uplifting programming rather than glorifying negative and degrading things. It also puts a high premium on educational programming for children, particularly during times of the day when kids are likely to watch television the most.

The arts are also a beautiful thing to behold. You can see paintings and sculpture and plays that lift us up rather than tear us down. All forms of music—country-western, alternative, rock and roll, classical—touch the depths of our souls and make us soar to new heights. The creative artists in this world inspire us to be better people—to love more, to laugh more, and to live better lives.

The Rugged Plains of Reality

Am I dreaming? Well, yes, I am. But it's nice sometimes to think about what heaven on earth might look like if it were actually possible. Unfortunately, we live on the rugged plains of reality. We don't live in a spiritual utopia. So, in light of that sobering fact, we'll have to swim back upstream to see what's really happening in our world today. We need to examine if, in fact, all of these entities are doing their parts to reinforce the same values the family is teaching, modeling, and living out in the parent-CEO family.

Before I launch into a litany of cultural facts and societal stats, let me explain why I'm presenting all of this information to you. Please understand it's not my intention to dump all of this stuff on you to make you feel fearful. Parts of our world *are* scary and stained with ugliness, but I believe in spite of the darkness that exists, there is great hope for the family. We can make a positive influence on the world around us. And we'll look at ways to do that later on in the chapter. But first, at the risk of sounding like a stereotypical pastor, I want to give you a taste of what the family today is up against. Again, don't be discouraged by what you are about to read. Keep in mind there is light at the end of the tunnel—and at the end of the chapter.

Art

First, let's go back to what the arts look like in the real world. Michael Medved, in his book *Hollywood Versus America,* exposes where some of our tax dollars are going in the "art" world. I won't go into the grim details—you can read them for yourself in his book—but it is truly sad what the National Endowment for the Arts and other institutions are supporting and passing off as art today. I'm really not trying to be critical, but most of the art these days—and I was an art major in college—does not inspire and enlighten the way it once did. A lot of the modern and postmodern art does nothing more than enrage the spirit. I heard someone say modern art is a conspiracy between rich people and artists to make the rest of us feel uncultured. I thought that was funny and sad at the same time, because the only uncultured people, in my opinion, are the ones buying and supporting a lot of the trash loosely labeled as art.

Music

Let's swim a little farther upstream into the realm of music. I want to spend more time here, because surely music will hold up its end of the deal in regard to family values. After all, music is so important, especially in the lives of our youth. And it, more than any other medium, affects the human soul. Let me begin by asking a question: if you are a music buff, can you name one song from three decades ago that encouraged sexual violence, incest, or rape? How about any songs that glorified robbery or the use of handguns in everyday life? Where is the music from that era that encouraged violence in various other prurient forms: cop killing, drive-by shootings, and gang violence. If you can do that, I'll be extremely surprised, because there were no songs like that thirty years ago.

Today, however, is another story entirely. Song after song encourages behavior like that I just mentioned. I am referring to a large number of rap, rock, and alternative groups today that our young people are exposed to regularly. I believe if most parents knew the kinds of lyrics their young people listen to daily, they would be shocked out of their minds. These songs are on the radio, on the CDs in your kids' bedrooms, and on music TV coming into your home.

MTV was created in 1981. It began as a curiosity but has become a cultural force. As of 2001, MTV's twentieth anniversary, more than 340 million homes worldwide were hooked into its music television.[1] (This number does not include other cable music-video channels like VH1 or CMT.)

Dr. James Dobson, psychologist, author, and radio personality with Focus on the Family, in his book *Bringing Up Boys* related the following about MTV:

> *Executives of MTV, with their emphasis on sex and violence, admit attempting to shape each generation of adolescents. One of their corporate ads pictures the back of a teenager's head with "MTV" shaved in his hair. The copy reads, "MTV is not a channel. It's a cultural force. People don't watch it, they love it. MTV has affected the way an entire generation thinks, talks, dresses and buys." The amazing thing about this ad is that MTV not only admits they are trying to manipulate the young and immature; they spend big bucks bragging about it.[2]*

I could name the actual groups I believe are harmful and quote lyrics from their songs, but I don't think that's necessary. For one thing, there are too many groups to list, and new ones pop up almost daily. Let me just encourage you strongly to know what your kids are listening to when you're not around. Take the CD jackets out and read the lyrics to these songs. It will sadden you to know what degrading influences are finding their way into the minds of our youth.

Anyone who tells you this stuff doesn't affect our kids is kidding you. There is a correlation between the things our children listen to and watch and their behavior. I don't need to cite scientific evidence for this. All we have to do is employ a little common sense. I liken the correlation between the intake of music and the arts and behavior to the correlation between eating a candy bar and gaining fifty pounds. If I ate one candy bar, would I gain fifty pounds? No. But if I decided to eat two hundred candy bars a day for thirty days, yes, I would gain fifty pounds. We can't expect our children to walk around wearing blinders and earplugs. But when we allow a constant, steady diet of this junk into their minds and hearts, it can and will change the trajectory of their lives and of your family. Parents, I can't make the call for you. You have to make the choice for your family. I have to be honest and tell it to you straight: it is evident that the music and the arts are not holding up their end of the bargain.

Television

Well, the arts and music have fallen down on the job. But surely other areas of the media—specifically television and movies—act responsibly, right? I mean, come on, there's so much power in the media I'm sure its members aren't taking this responsibility lightly. Think again!

On the evening of the Super Bowl game in January 2004, all of America was shocked at a half-time show that immediately sparked a national debate on public decency. Following the crotch-grabbing, hip-gyrating, flag-desecrating, breast-baring tidal wave that CBS, the NFL, and MTV served to one sixth of the world à la Justin Timberlake, Janet Jackson, and friends, the national breath was knocked out of our lungs. According to *USA Today,* 7.8 million children were watching the game during the time frame of the half-time show.[3]

I have to ask, though, why were we so shocked? The Super Bowl spectacle was just the inevitable outcome of an entertainment medium that has been spinning out of control for quite some time.

In 1996 *U.S. News & World Report* had a research team look at a week of prime-time television in mid-March.[4] Here is what they found after surveying the programming of ABC, CBS, NBC, and Fox: the number one rated show at the time devoted episodes to themes such as oral sex, masturbation, homosexuality, and orgasms. Again, this was prime-time programming over eight years ago as of the publication of this book.

These *U.S. News* researchers logged a sexual act or sexual reference every four minutes on prime-time television. The article went on to say that portrayals of premarital sex during prime time outnumbered sex within marriage eight to one.

In addition to the number of sexual scenes and references, over a sixty-minute time frame an average of fifty crimes and twelve murders were committed. They also cited this statistic: the average child and teenager watch approximately twenty-two hours of television a week. How many young eyes have witnessed these harmful images over the course of their twenty-two hours of television watching during a week's time? And how much worse has it gotten since 1996? I think that question was answered by Janet and Justin on February 1, 2004, in Houston.

Consider also the new line of so-called reality TV that has taken television viewing to a new extreme. *USA Today* recently printed a feature article on the sex-soaked slate of reality shows that are anything but true to life.[5] On *The Bachelor*, a single guy simultaneously dates a harem of girls, methodically eliminating them until he finds his "perfect" match. So perfect, in fact, that only one of the couples from *The Bachelor* or *The Bachelorette* has led to marriage. And what about *Temptation Island*, the show that tempts four engaged couples with twenty-eight "sexy singles" whose sole charge is to try to get these engaged men and women to cheat on their husbands- and wives-to-be?

Let's not forget TV's first gay dating show, *Boy Meets Boy,* which gives one homosexual male the opportunity to choose from among fifteen men, by process of elimination, to accompany him on an exotic vacation. The "twist," according to the show's creator, is that some of the men in the group are actually straight.

Even those participating and consulting in these shows see how degrading they are to our culture. The same *USA Today* article quoted Dr. Drew Pinsky, a health and relationship expert, on CBS's reality show *Big Brother.* He said, "These shows are getting meaner and more dramatic and more chaotic and more destructive." The article went on to say, again in Pinsky's words, "Not only are today's dating shows vicious . . . but they're also only getting worse by appealing to viewers' baser instincts."[6] That, in a nutshell, is the reality of reality TV. One article said that "reality shows have actually become the new family television."[7] If that's the case, we're in sad shape. As a culture, we are not rising to new levels; we are sinking to new lows.

Here's the rugged reality of what's being served on TV. Sadly, TV moguls for the most part have abdicated their responsibility in upholding family values. Even with a renewed national debate on television decency, they claim they are just feeding the monster. They defend their actions by giving excuses like, "We're just dishing up what the viewing public wants to watch." So, parents, don't count on the television industry to come alongside you in your quest for wholesome entertainment.

Movies

How about the movies coming out of Hollywood? One of the most popular movies during the summer of 2003 was *American Wedding,* the third of the *American Pie* trilogy of movies. According to family movie review Web sites such as Screenit.com and Previewonline.org, this one movie contained an excess of fifty f-words, thirty-two s-words, and twenty-three slang terms for male/female genitalia, in addition to a host of other profanity.[8] The sexual content was labeled as extreme and highly inappropriate.[9]

I think you get the idea. The movies available to our youth are as bad or worse than much of what they see on TV. This is just one movie, but it represents the kind of fare Hollywood is marketing to our teenagers in particular. It does come with an R rating, but that isn't stopping teens from seeing it and other movies like it—in droves.

At this point, I must steal a quote from a cartoon poster boy for the kid-CEO family—TV's own Bart Simpson. In one episode of *The Simpsons,* Bart told his father, "You know, it is just hard not listening to the movies and television. They have spent more time raising me than you have." I hope you see we cannot let the electronic media, the electronic baby-sitters, teach values to our children. Don't let the entertainment industry fool you, because for the most part it simply has no values.

The pressure is mounting on the American family at breakneck pace. But hang on, because we're not through yet.

The Internet

Let's talk about the Internet, this supposedly wonderful technological tool that has come into our lives. The Internet, despite many of its obvious benefits as far as commerce and research and convenience, has also become a vast depository of pornographic and violent material. Internetfilterreview.com compiles statistics on the Internet every year to help keep parents aware of what's out there on the World Wide Web. In

2003 they found 4.2 million pornographic Web sites on the Internet, with 72 million people visiting them annually. In addition, $2.5 billion is spent every year on cyberporn.[10]

The stats on children and the Internet will break your heart. Again according to Internetfilterreview.com, 90 percent of eight- to sixteen-year-olds have viewed pornography online, most of them while doing homework. Fifteen- to seventeen-year-olds have had multiple hard-core experiences while surfing the Web, and the largest consumers of Internet porn are children in the twelve-to-seventeen age group.[11] According to the National Coalition for the Protection of Children and Families, the average age at which children are first exposed to porn is now age eight, down from an earlier average of age eleven. And 80 percent of those exposures are accidental.[12]

I haven't even addressed the other dangers on the Web, such as sites that instruct you how to commit suicide or how to make bombs. Or terrorist-group sites that target our children with anti-American messages. Or the hundreds of violent video games accessible to our children on the Web—the same kinds of games as, and sometimes far worse than, those found on home game systems and in shopping-mall arcades.

I think it's clear enough that there's a world of content on the Internet that does not support the transcendent values we want for our families. The Internet can be a wonderful tool, but don't be fooled. Be a discerning parent and know the dangers available to your children with the click of a mouse or at the touch of a keyboard.

The Government

Before we get too depressed, let's swim a little farther upstream and take a look at the government on the rugged plains of reality. Perhaps our government of the people, by the people, and for the people is doing a better job than these other cultural elements in supporting family values. On a bright note, I do see some great men and women in leadership positions in our government today, but they are great only insofar as they lead according to God's values. You will find in the Old Testament books of the Bible a recurring theme regarding earthly leaders: those leaders who did what was right in the eyes of God prospered, and the people turned their faces toward God. Sadly, though, you will also see another recurring theme in the Old Testament: those leaders who did what was right in their own eyes, and consequently what was evil in the sight of the Lord, did not prosper, and the people turned their faces away from God.

So much potential for good exists in our great country. Despite the conscientious, moral leaders, many of the people who wield the power are not living up to that potential. Just recently, in the state of Alabama, a federal judge ordered the Alabama chief justice to remove a plaque of the Ten Commandments from the lobby of the Alabama Supreme Court Building. He gave this order despite the fact that Alabama's state constitution specifically upholds God's divine law as the underpinning of the state's laws, a constitution the chief justice swore an oath to protect and defend, and despite the fact that 77 percent of Americans supported the Ten Commandments display.[13]

What else has our government brought about lately? I was in the midst of writing this chapter when I heard a news report that the courts are also paving a way for teenage girls to have abortions performed during the school day without either parental permission or parental consent. As if abortion were not easy enough already, our judicial system has made it possible for frightened girls who have made a big mistake to make an even bigger one without even having the opportunity to receive counsel from their own parents.

On another front, in an affront to the traditional meaning of marriage and family, gay marriage is gaining acceptance at the state and federal level following a ruling by federal judges that state sodomy laws are unconstitutional. And the Massachusetts Supreme Court ruled in February 2004 that the state must grant marriage rights to same-sex couples, intensifying nationwide debates to codify the definition of marriage as between a man and woman in state constitutions and our federal Constitution.

Even the words "under God" in our pledge of allegiance have come under attack, and the Supreme Court is set to rule, as I write this, whether these words are constitutional. The words "full faith and trust of the United States Government" are holding less and less water these days. We need not let the political pundits kid us, because the government fails in many areas related to the kind of values we want to impart to our children.

The Marketplace

Let's continue swimming upstream and talk about what's happening in the marketplace. Corporate scandals have rocked our culture over the last several years. Companies such as Enron and WorldCom looked great on the outside, with beautiful buildings and glowing annual reports, but on the inside things were not so great. Packed deep inside the walls of these powerhouses of money and commerce were stores of lies, deception, and greed. If you research business journals, you will readily discover that the scandals we're uncovering are just the tip of the corporate iceberg. Employees and their families have lost their entire pensions, not to mention their jobs, as a result of the lack of integrity in business.

And what about the idea of putting family before business? Money has taken precedence over the value of people, which means that while job responsibilities have increased, compensation has remained stagnant or actually decreased. According to *USA Today*, corporations are cutting back on family-friendly benefits, like flex-time, full-time commuting, and adoption assistance, because these benefits are too costly and no longer needed to retain workers.[14] Parents who work are pressured to spend more time at the office to compete with those who don't have kids and are able to work longer hours. It's pretty tough to be a parent these days.

Education

How about education? The public schools have to do their job, too. Up to this point, it appears that parenting has become a solo act. Are the school systems helping the situation any?

The public school systems say they are into "values-free educating." It sounds so sophisticated, so erudite. But there is no such thing as "values-free" anything. Professor William Kilpatrick in his book *Why Johnny Can't Tell Right from Wrong* says that instead of teaching morality, schools claim they are helping children discover values by consensus or a personal decision-making process. This way they are communicating that no one value has more merit than another.[15]

However, Kilpatrick goes on to observe this about values education in schools: "For students, it has meant wholesale confusion about moral values: learning to question values they have scarcely acquired, unlearning values taught at home, and concluding that questions of right and wrong are always merely subjective."[16]

Can we trust the public school systems to teach morality to our children, when they are not allowed to recognize any final authority for what is right and wrong? Can we trust them to teach sex education, when all sexual orientations and levels of sexual activity are treated as equally valid and morally neutral? While abstinence-based sex education is making a comeback, it still is presented only as one of many options.[17]

Now, don't get me wrong, there are some great schools out there with great classrooms and phenomenal teachers. And to their credit, many schools have made sex education and other values-related programs voluntary. That means, though, we need to pay attention to the curriculum and pull our kids if we feel the material being presented doesn't fall in line with the values we teach in the home.

Don't Give Up! Principles for Change

In light of this abdication of responsibility among cultural influences, take a look—a long look—at what is left. We end up with a little autonomous family alone against the world. Are you wondering, as a parent, why you feel so discouraged? Do you wonder why you feel depressed at times? Do you sometimes feel frightened about the future of your family? Look at what you're up against. God did not intend it to be this way, but this is exactly what we've brought on ourselves as a society.

The question at this point is: what do we do? The future may look a little bleak. The graphs are going south. The stats are scary. But don't despair; there is hope for the family and for culture. We have a ray of sunshine available to us—the same light that has always been there. We have the Bible, God's Word for all time and all places. And any time the Bible is operative in the world, there is hope for humankind. We can look forward to a positive future for the family when we get serious about this dynamic, life-changing book.

With that in mind, I want to suggest several principles that can truly change the trajectory of your life, your family, and the culture in which we live—because we can change the culture one life at a time and one family at a time.

Whether you're married or a single parent, I ask you to consider these things to help counter cultural influences. I believe these suggestions, if you follow them, can and will have a phenomenal and indelible impact on your family.

Ask Critical Questions

First, ask yourself, "Are my family's entertainment choices based on true and lasting guidelines?" Consider these words from the Bible as a standard for what your family listens to, watches, and participates in: "Fix your thoughts on what is true and honorable and right. Think about things that are pure and lovely and admirable. Think about things that are excellent and worthy of praise" (Phil. 4:8). Every time you buy a video, purchase a CD, walk into the movie theater, turn on the TV and channel surf, or log onto the Internet, ask yourself if what you're about to see, hear, and participate in fits those biblical guidelines.

We say, as parents, we want to teach values. We say we want to have a parent-CEO household that models transcendent principles. Too often, though, there is a major disconnect between what we say and what we actually do. If we say one thing to our kids and then do another, we can forget about our kids or our culture kidding us; we are kidding ourselves. Removing that kind of hypocrisy from our lives is going to involve some serious decision-making power, both on our part and on our children's. Living the hypocrisy-free life will involve removing, in a loving way, a lot of trash to which our families are currently being exposed.

I emphasize that this needs to be done in a firm yet loving way, because coming down on your kids with a harsh, judgmental tone regarding the things they listen to and watch will push them away from you and the values you want for them. Sit down with them and explain that you, as Mom and Dad, have been given the responsibility to make some hard choices for the family. And those choices include music, movies, TV, art, the Internet, and school activities.

It will mean installing software on the family computer that blocks objectionable material from the Internet, and it may mean personally monitoring all of your children's Internet access. It will mean actually using the parental controls that come with your cable or satellite service, and it may mean removing cable TV all together. It will mean missing out on many of the movies coming out of Hollywood. It will mean rejecting outright the majority of popular music. It may also mean excluding your kids from certain school activities or classes that don't match up with your values. You will have to decide, against the backdrop of these biblical guidelines, what is appropriate for your family and what is not. Are you ready for that? It's going to take some incredible courage on your part to go against the flow of our culture. But I'm here to tell you it can be done.

Here's what will happen, though, as you begin to weed out the negative influences that have been allowed to grow wild in the family yard. The fertile soil will be rich with opportunity for new growth. You can plant the seeds of things that are true, honorable, right, pure, lovely, admirable, excellent, and worthy of praise. If you're discerning and wise, you can find some good stuff for your family. For instance, some producers out there are making movies that uphold family values. And a fair number of quality shows are making their way onto the small screen as well.

Newsweek observed, and rightly so, that in the midst of the current cultural cries against entertainment indecency, "there's tons of family programming. . . . There are dozens of excellent family shows, probably more than ever." "The problem," the article noted later on, ". . . is knowing where to look."[18] Parents, it's going to take some time and effort to find quality entertainment for your family, but it's out there. You just have to make the determined choice to allow into your home only those forms of entertainment that match your values as a family. You can choose not to buy what the entertainment industry is producing.

I also want to emphasize the choices you need to make on the musical front, because music is such a huge influence among our young people. As Christian parents desiring to establish a parent-CEO household, you need to open up your family to burgeoning choices in Christian music. If you like rap, funk, jazz, alternative, or rock and roll, there is excellent Christian music that communicates uplifting lyrics.

Second, ask yourself, "What core values are transmitted through my family's entertainment choices?" Sit down as a family, as you feel it is age-appropriate for your child or student, and discuss the lyrics of a top-forty song together. Watch a current block-buster movie and discuss its content. Tape *Friends* or another popular sitcom and talk about it, scene by scene.

For instance, here's a scene from an early *Friends* episode that would provide great conversational material with older kids: Phoebe has a problem. Her new boyfriend won't sleep with her. Her friend Joey says, "The guy still won't put out, huh?" Later in the show Phoebe is very excited because she finally "made it" with her boyfriend. The trick, she explains, was to make it clear to him that she wasn't expecting a commitment just because they had had sex. Joey says, "You mean he got you to agree to regular sex without a commitment? Wow! This guy is my god."

As you discuss scenes like this one from TV shows or movies, or lyrics from popular songs, ask your children questions like these: "Kids, what values are being taught here? Are they reinforcing the values we teach in our home?" Or "How does this lyric, this dialogue, this action, contradict what the Bible teaches?" And do something that the music industry and Hollywood rarely do: talk about the consequences of living the kind of lifestyles portrayed in these songs, movies, and TV shows. Talk about what happens after you take the drug, after you live out the violence, after you engage in self-destructive behavior, or after you have sex outside the commitment of marriage. Sit down and watch MTV or VH1 with them and point out the reality that about 85 percent of that stuff glorifies drug use, sex, violence, or rebellion without showing the deadly consequences.

Then take your kids to the Bible and communicate the truth that exposes the lies of our culture. Following are some verses you might want to use in your discussions:

- I will refuse to look at anything vile and vulgar. I hate all crooked dealings; I will have nothing to do with them. (Ps. 101:3)

- So put to death the sinful, earthly things lurking within you. Have nothing to do with sexual sin, impurity, lust, and shameful desires. Don't be greedy for the good things of this life, for that is idolatry. (Col. 3:5)

- If your sinful nature controls your mind, there is death. But if the Holy Spirit controls your mind, there is life and peace. (Rom. 8:6)

- Run from anything that stimulates youthful lust. Follow anything that makes you want to do right. Pursue faith and love and peace, and enjoy the companionship of those who call on the Lord with pure hearts. (2 Tim. 2:22)

- Run away from sexual sin! No other sin so clearly affects the body as this one does. For sexual immorality is a sin against your own body. Or don't you know that your body is the temple of the Holy Spirit, who lives in you and was given to you by God? You do not belong to yourself, for God bought you with a high price. So you must honor God with your body. (1 Cor. 6:18–20)

- The lips of an immoral woman are as sweet as honey, and her mouth is smoother than oil. But the result is as bitter as poison, sharp as a double-edged sword. Her feet go down to death; her steps lead straight to the grave. (Prov. 5:3–5)

- Whoever walks with the wise will become wise; whoever walks with fools will suffer harm. (Prov. 13:20)

Make the Church Your Family's Epicenter

I talked about this in the last chapter, but I must repeat it here. The second major thing you need to do to counter the culture is to make the church a major priority in your household. I may be biased about this point because I'm a pastor, but what other entity is going to assist you in teaching your children core values? I think we've seen adequate evidence so far that families aren't getting the help they need from any other segment of society. I thank God for the creativity we have in the children's and youth ministry of our church. We have men and women who are committed to teaching the truth in an age-appropriate, creative, and compelling way, but more important, in a biblical way.

If you aren't excited about going to church, find a church that excites you. And let me say something else you will rarely hear from a pastor: if you consistently hear a boring message in church, do not blame the message; blame the messenger. The church should be the most dynamic place you visit. The message you hear may not always be comfortable, because sometimes we have to address difficult topics. But it should always be creative, compelling, and relevant to your life. I know for a fact many churches like that exist, because I have spoken to hundreds of church leaders across the country who are committed to guiding their churches that way. Do some research, ask around, and find a church that will help you bring up your family in these dangerous cultural times.

Lisa and I have unashamedly relied on our church to help

rear our children. As we look around society and see how the dominoes are falling, we understand more than ever the importance of loading up on what the church has to offer. We fill up on the front end of the week, knowing what's coming from our culture the rest of the week.

Since we're emphasizing a parent-CEO household, I have to call parents to task on this. It is our responsibility as the leaders of the home to make sure our children are in church. If you are asking your kids, "Do you want to go to church today?" then you are blowing it. If you are allowing them to whine and complain their way out of attending, you are missing it. Let's be honest. There are times when they will not want to go to church and will instead throw out excuses like "I don't like the other kids" or "I don't feel like going" or "I don't have any fun there." But church should not be an option. It is not an option for my kids, and it was not an option when I was growing up.

As a kid, I was heavily involved in basketball. I even had the opportunity to play Division I at Florida State (well, actually, I rode the bench). Yet through all of the basketball I played and the other athletics I was involved in, my parents never allowed me to miss the beauty and the joy of the local church. The church, not athletics, is what has given me the octane to live a life full of meaning and purpose.

It always excites me to hear my kids talk about what they have learned in church and to see the relationships they are developing there. When I hand them over to the nursery, preschool, children's church, and youth leaders, I can be thankful that our church is reinforcing the transcendent values we try to teach, model, inspire, and live out in our home.

Are you experiencing that same excitement? Are you leading

your kids in this area? If not, you need to begin this week to give church the priority it deserves in the family agenda.

Know Your Children's Companions

When you see the word *companions,* you probably think of your children's friends. And that's definitely part of the equation. You need to know who their friends are. Whom are they hanging out with on the weekends? Whom are they talking with on the phone every night? Whom are they going to movies and concerts with?

The Bible tells us a companion of fools will suffer harm (Prov. 13:20). That's a good warning for parent and child alike. Get to know your children's friends by having them over for dinner, allowing them to spend the weekend for a sleepover, or inviting them on camping trips or to the local amusement park for the day. These peer influences are likely to have just as much (or more) impact on your child's moral development as you have, so it's critical that you know who they are and what they stand for.

But this idea of companions goes beyond human friendships. It also includes the electronic, visual, auditory, and emotional companions of your children. We've already addressed many of these in the preceding pages—how much time the average child spends watching TV, MTV, and movies, listening to CDs, and surfing the Web. Statistics bear out that these electronic friends spend more time with your children than you do. According to researcher George Barna, eight- to thirteen-year-olds average nearly forty-eight hours per week of mass media intake, compared to only thirty-one hours spent with Mom and twenty-three spent with Dad. And many of the hours kids spend with parents these days, Barna observed, are in the car, darting from one activity to another.[19] Are you aware of the influence these mass media companions have on your children? What kinds of values are these electronic friends teaching your kids? Chances are, based on what we've looked at so far in this chapter, they're teaching values contradictory to your own.

The parent-CEO family knows about and guards against those cultural companions that, as the Bible says, can cause our children to "suffer harm." It's your job, Mom and Dad, to protect your children. It is your job to be discerning and wise about who and what influences your kids. It's your job to make those tough choices about their media intake. Don't leave that up to your children, because they are waiting and begging for you to make the call in this area.

Parents, the bottom line is we must stay engaged with what culture is conveying to our kids through these various mediums of entertainment. Take to heart this observation from the pages of *Time* magazine in an article entitled, "Who's in Charge Here?": "Parents who give up and back off leave their children at the mercy of a merciless culture. The ones who stand firm and stay involved often find their families grow closer."[20] We can't isolate our children from cultural influences, but we can help them navigate the maze by making the most discerning choices available to us.

Read Together

One last principle I want to suggest briefly as a way to communicate your values in a sometimes antagonistic culture is to read quality books with your children. Set aside regular time to read stories that embody the character qualities you want for your family. First of all, read from the Bible together, about Abraham, Joseph, Moses, David, Paul, and all of the other heroes of the faith. And then pick up other great stories that communicate character qualities like honesty, integrity, courage, and compassion. Read the classics. Read fables and fairy tales. Read biographies of principled individuals from different periods in history. You won't believe how these stories will inspire your kids to be better people and to do great things.

I again cite the work of William Kilpatrick, who writes in his book *Why Johnny Can't Tell Right from Wrong,* "[Stories] allow us to identify with models of courage and virtue in a way that 'problem solving' does not." He goes on in the next paragraph, "Stories supply examples of virtue in action; they can supply strength and wisdom as well."[21] Kilpatrick offers an extensive reading guide for children in each age group in the final chapter of his book. The book is worth it just for that list, which includes great works like *The Children's Bible in 365 Stories,* the *Little House* series, *The Hobbit,* and *The Chronicles of Narnia.*[22] Also consider *The Book of Virtues* and *The Children's Book of Virtues,* which are compilations of timeless moral stories from around the world. Both books are by former Secretary of Education William Bennett.

Make a Difference

The information in this chapter may seem overwhelming to you. Writing it has been overwhelming and discouraging at times. It may seem to you that the whole world is against us, and there is nothing we can do with our little families to make a difference. Or you may get the feeling that our culture is falling apart at the seams, and we just need to accept that. Despite all of the problems and negative influences we see in our culture today, I am still optimistic about the family.

Many parents are making a difference in their families by sacrificing financially to put their children in private schools where they will learn transcendent values. Other parents are home-schooling their children for the same reason. Still others have gotten involved, elbow deep, in the public school system to help make positive changes in that often difficult environment. It takes guts and courage to educate your children in each of these unique arenas. It takes parents who are willing to make a difference in their corner of the world.

That is how change is going to take place in our society. Positive change occurs when normal, average, everyday people like you and me stand up and make a difference. Whether you're a school principal, a college professor, the owner of a large corporation or small company, a homemaker, a retail clerk, a factory worker, or a computer technician, ask yourself how you can make a difference in your corner of the world.

Whatever your circles of influence, whether it is in the school system, the workplace, the government, the media, or the arts and music, you need to stand up and say, "I am going to reinforce those transcendent values taught, modeled, and lived out in the family." If each one of us will strategically focus on the area or areas that we have the greatest passion for and the greatest pull in, together we can impact the culture in a positive way. Just imagine what could happen if every concerned parent, wherever he is and whoever he is, got serious about making a difference in his corner of the world.

Before I end this chapter, I want you to remember one final principle from the pages of the Bible that impacts your family's future. Paul wrote the following words in the New Testament Book of Galatians to a group of tired, worn-out Christians: "Let us not get tired of doing what is right, for after a while we will reap a harvest of blessing if we don't get discouraged and give up" (Gal. 6:9 TLB). Single mom, don't get discouraged. Single dad, don't give up. Working mom and working dad, keep doing what you know to be right. And you will reap the rewards someday. It may not seem like it now, in the heat of the battle, but good things will come to those who persevere.

Are you ready to stand up to a culture that seems to be set on tearing your family apart? In the face of opposition, are you ready to say, "As for me and my house, we are going to serve the Lord"? Are you ready to use true and lasting guidelines to evaluate your family's entertainment choices? Are you ready to take a long, hard, serious look at the values being taught in the media, in music and the arts, and discuss those with your children? Are you ready to make a commitment to a local church, to make it the epicenter of your family's life? Are you ready to go into your corner of the world and make a positive difference?

I truly hope so. It's time to say as parents that we're not going to remain under the influence of the culture. Rather, we need to make a choice to be the influencers of our society by modeling God's values.

PART THREE

Intimacy

Keeping the
Love Alive During
the Parenting Years

{ 5 }

A Current Affair

STROLL WITH ME through the average day of a typical subur-banite. This person wakes up, gets dressed, grabs some breakfast, pets the dog, sets his burglar alarm, unlocks his car, gets in, locks his car, and drives to the office. When he gets to the office, he removes his security card from his wallet, swipes it, and greets the security guard. He knows he has to work hard over the next several hours because later that day he has to hop on a plane for an important business meeting.

He zips to the airport, gets out of his car, locks it and en-gages the alarm, walks into the airport, presents his ID at the security checkpoint, empties his pockets of his keys, wallet, and cell phone, unpacks his laptop to be screened, puts his bag on the conveyor belt to be x-rayed, and then walks through the metal detector. He gathers up all of his belongings, puts them all back where they came from, and heads to the gate for departure. He presents his ID once again to the gate agent. As he boards the plane, he knows there's a good chance an air marshal is on board for added security. He arrives at his destination without complication and completes his business. He heads back to the airport and then repeats the same drill on the way home.

When he walks to his car in the parking garage at the airport, it's already nightfall. He looks around for any suspicious characters. He disengages his alarm, gets in, locks the car, drives home, pulls up in front of his home, gets out, locks the car, and engages the alarm. He then unlocks the door to his home and greets his wife and two kids, who have been eagerly awaiting his arrival. It's been a long day and his kids are already dressed for bed, so he gives them big hugs and kisses good night. He then pets his German Shepherd guard dog and turns on the television to relax for a few minutes before retiring for the night.

While perusing the pages of the newspaper, he also watches the evening news. The paper and the news confirm each other. There's another child kidnapping and another suicide bombing in the Middle East. The news, as usual, is pretty scary. Before going to bed, he checks the locks on the windows and the deadbolts on the doors. He engages his home security system and then checks on his kids. He completes his nightly routine, kisses his wife good night, and puts his head on the pillow for another peaceful night's sleep.

This scenario typifies a society saturated with security. Everywhere we look, we run into security issues. Apartment complexes, neighborhoods, and businesses are being constructed with security in mind. They have walls around the property, guards to check incoming vehicles, and sophisticated, intricate alarm systems. We install the Club on the steering wheels of our cars and LoJack devices to track vehicles if they're stolen. The movie *Panic Room*, starring Jodie Foster, demonstrated the highly secure rooms that some people have built as a safe retreat if someone invades their homes. Americans spend millions and millions of dollars each year to install and maintain redundant systems to protect their property and lives.

Physically we go to great lengths to secure our families against being victims of the rising crime rate. But I need to ask a critical question: *what are we doing to protect our families from being violated by something much more insidious? Something that attacks from the inside—the scourge of infidelity?* What measures are we taking to keep adulterous affairs from ravaging our lives, our families, and our homes? How do we protect our marriages and our children from the rising rate of adultery?

The statistics on adultery are staggering. Thirty-seven percent of all men report they have had at least one affair while married. Twenty-nine percent of women admit to infidelity in marriage.[1] That means that nearly one out of three people has been unfaithful in marriage. It's obvious we have a security breach in the family. But what can we do about it? How do we protect ourselves from the devastating effects of adultery? Again, the thought may be resurfacing in your mind, "I thought this was a book about parenting. Why is he writing about marriage?" Yes, this is a parenting book, but I hope you have already taken to heart the critical importance of the marriage relationship in the home. We must protect our marriages if we want to protect our families. The strength of your marriage will be the strength of your family. Adultery affects kids as much as or more than it does adults. If you love your kids, you must conscientiously, intentionally, and jealously protect your household from the havoc a broken home causes.

With that in mind, I want to present in this chapter several challenges to both husbands and wives to help guard against infidelity. I believe when you do these two things, you will be on your way to guarding your heart and your home from destruction. I simply ask you to take the same care in protecting the sanctity of your marriage and family as you do in protecting your physical property and life.

If you are single, don't flip to the next chapter or the next section of the book. I will be addressing married men and women primarily in the next two chapters, but even as a single parent, you must commit yourself to sexual purity and to the sanctity of the home for your own good and the good of your children. And I'm referring to both your single days and if you should marry again. If or when you enter into a marriage relationship again (or perhaps for the first time), you need to have already committed yourself proactively to the principles outlined in this chapter. Don't wait until you are in a compromising position, such as a temptation to have an affair with a married person or to engage in premarital sex with another single adult, to make the right decision. I realize this is not a popular stance to take, but I promise you that God's way is always the best way, in sex, in marriage, in dating, and in every other avenue of life.

Become Security Guards

The first thing you must do, husbands and wives, if you are going to affair-proof your home, is become security guards. Good security guards are men and women who are alert. They don't go to sleep on the job and they never let down their guard. The ultimate security guards are people who patrol every square inch of their marital property. They know what's going on at all times. In fact, the Bible tells us, "Be careful! Watch out for attacks from the Devil, your great enemy. He prowls around like a roaring lion, looking for some victim to devour" (1 Pet. 5:8).

I've known husbands and wives who have said, "There's no way an affair could happen to us. That is impossible. We are completely protected." But I've also seen those same couples fall by the wayside because either the wife or the husband neglected the role of a security guard.

Lisa and I, early in our marriage, used to baby-sit for a family who had their own security guard. Twenty-four hours a day, seven days a week, a guard sat in front of their estate and checked every car that slowed down by or turned into the property. Whether it was the team that cleaned the yard, the garden, or the pool, a guest, or a family member, a security guard was watching. And at night, the night-watch guard drove around the grounds two or three times with a giant spotlight to check out the gardens, the pool, the wall, and the wing to make sure everything was safe and secure. In addition to security guards, this mansion also had an intricate alarm system I could never figure out.

Husbands, wives, when you patrol your property, you also need to use a giant light to keep yourself, your marriage, and your family from harm. I am referring to the light of God's truth that he has given us in the Bible. Shine it in your eyes, shine it in your mind, shine it on your bodies, shine it on your relationships, and make sure everything you do matches up to what God wants for your life. Does every activity and relationship reflect his beauty, honor, and holiness? In essence, what we need to do is to guard our hearts, because the heart represents the totality of our beings. Proverbs 4:23 puts it this way: "Above all else, guard your heart, for it affects everything you do." From the heart comes everything we do, say, and feel.

An important part of a security guard's job is to monitor all the vehicles coming into the property. When we drive up to many apartment complexes and gated neighborhoods, the security guard walks out and says, "Stop. Tell me your names, please." We give him our names. He walks to the back of the car and records our license plate number.

"Who would you like to see?"

We tell him. He turns and walks into the guard shack, picks up the phone, and calls the party we named. If the party says, "Yes, let them in," then he says, "Okay, come on in," and we drive through. If the party is not in or doesn't want to see us, the guard says, "I'm sorry, you will have to turn around."

Adultery begins not in the bedroom, but in our hearts and minds. The precursors of an affair start in the head and heart long before you get in bed with a third party. If we're the ultimate security guards in our marriages, we have to stand by the gate as thoughts and emotions request access to our hearts. When they try to get in, we need to lower the security arm and ask, "What is the purpose of your visit? Why are you trying to gain access?" We need to be very careful, ask questions, and write down license plate numbers. If a particular thought or feeling or relationship does not glorify God, if a lustful thought could lead us astray, we need to say, "I'm sorry, you'll need to turn around. Turn around and get out of town."

Security guards, the battle is in our hearts and in our minds.

We cannot let these adulterous thoughts come in; if we do, they will begin to mess with us. They whisper lies to us: "Hey, see that girl [guy] over there? I know this is outlandish, but what would it be like to have lunch alone with her [him]? I know you want to do it. What would it be like to hold that person? I know there's no way you'll do it, but it won't hurt just to fantasize about it." The temptation to think thoughts like these is not a sin, but it becomes a sin when we allow those thoughts access and begin to nurture them. It's what we do with those thoughts that turns them into sins against our spouse and against God.

Lust occurs when we see someone of the opposite sex and not only appreciate his or her beauty, but also begin to undress and perform sexual acts with him or her in our minds. That is lust. Sexual thoughts are a part of our lives; we are sexual beings. For instance, speaking from the male point of view, I've heard it said that men have one sexual thought every thirty minutes. I've also heard that they have one every thirty seconds. The truth is probably somewhere in between. Regardless of the statistics, the point is those thoughts are destined to come into our minds on a regular basis. If they are temptations in regard to sexuality, close the guard gate. Tell them to leave. And then refocus that sexual energy where it should be—on your spouse. The important thing is that you keep yourself clean and pure as you continuously check those incoming thoughts and feelings.

Install an Eight-Alarm Security System

You may be thinking, "Wait a minute. A security guard? That's all I have to be to guard against infidelity?" No, that is just the first level of security. There are still ways that thoughts and feelings can sneak in, over the wall or through the shrubs, to rob the sanctity of your marriage. Just like that home where Lisa and I baby-sat, we need redundant devices beyond the protection of a security guard to fully protect our marriages. That's why husbands and wives must install a second level of protection in their marital mansions. This is what I call an eight-alarm security system.

1. Beware When You Compare

The first alarm we must install in this eight-alarm security system is the Beware When You Compare alarm. Our entire world is into comparing. We compare waistlines, physiques, bank accounts, cars, clothes, vacations, schools, and even our kids and our spouses. It's unfair to compare, because when God made you and me, he threw out the comparison game. And when he brought you and your spouse together, he made a union that is one of a kind.

If you sense yourself starting to compare your life, your marriage, or your family with someone else's, the alarm should go off. Husbands and wives, do not compare your marriage with any other marriage. Yours is utterly unique. When you make comparisons, it's like going around and around in a re-volving door. You are making a lot of motion and commotion, but you're essentially going nowhere. Don't make statements like these: "Why don't you treat me the way she treats him?" or "I wish you looked like he does," or "I wish you could wear your hair the way she does." By comparing your husband or wife with someone else, you're making a mockery, a joke, of God's creation. Just think—if you weren't you, there would be a hole in history, a gap in creativity. So be yourself and don't expect your spouse to be someone else. Install the Beware When You Compare alarm.

2. Your Eyes Can Lead to Your Demise

John Maxwell, a best-selling author of several books on leadership and business ethics, once said the true character of a man is measured when he is alone in a hotel room. Think about it. That statement holds true for men and women alike. Our character is measured by what we do when no one else is looking. What movies do we watch? What TV shows do we choose? What magazines do we look at? What phone calls do we make? What books do we read? Whose company do we keep?

A couple of years ago my own character was tested in this way. On that occasion, I had an opportunity to lead a group of 108 people to the Holy Land, as I have done several times over the years. Another staff member came with me as a coleader, and we thoroughly enjoyed our time there. I taught at the different historical and biblical sights, and it was really an incredible spiritual high to walk where Jesus walked. I hope, one day, when the world settles down, to be able to take more trips to the Middle East.

On the return trip, I had to leave a day early to fly back to Dallas so I could speak in the four weekend services our church was running at the time. The other pastor had to stay with the group, so I flew by myself from Tel Aviv to Frankfurt and spent the night there. Then I flew from Frankfurt to Dallas/Fort Worth, cleared customs, drove to Fellowship Church, changed clothes in my office, and spoke four times with jet lag. It was a wild experience, to say the least.

One of the policies that the church board of trustees has set forth is that I never travel alone (we'll address that later in the chapter), but on this occasion I did travel alone due to the scheduling demands. It was an unsettling experience, I must say, to travel by myself to a place I had never been to or seen before. I was alone on the plane, exhausted from the trip. I had not seen Lisa in two weeks. I was coming off of a spiritual high. And to top it all off, I was preparing to speak four times when I landed in Dallas. To put it mildly, I was emotionally drained.

I knew when we landed in Frankfurt that the hotel I was staying in was going to be a temptation for me. If you know anything about Germany, you know the television over there is very sexually explicit. They show X-rated stuff right there on broadcast television for anyone to see. In all honesty, I felt the temptation to watch that stuff. The remote was right there on the bedside table. I was alone. No one was looking and no one knew me in Frankfurt, Germany. I could have done whatever I wanted to do and no one would have been the wiser.

I felt a tremendous tug-of-war taking place in my heart and mind. I remember meditating on some words from the Bible, and I remember submitting myself to God at that moment. I prayed, "God, I feel the temptation. I feel the trial. And I welcome it now because I know you are going to build some great character in my life. I am going to look past the temptation to what you are going to do."

Do you know what happened? Because of the power of God, not my own, I never even turned on the television. Is it because Ed Young is some great guy, some spiritual giant? No. I am a sinner, a rank-and-file person like everyone else. But I had resolved ahead of time not to defile myself with pornographic images, and because of the power of God I was able to keep that resolution. I knew what came through the eyes could eventually lead to my demise and that of my marriage, my family, and my career as a pastor and author. The stakes were high. But when I saw Lisa that weekend in Dallas, I had no guilt. When I preached the message that weekend, God used it in an incredible way.

Do you have some movies, some videos, a few romance novels or magazines lurking in your bedroom or in a locked closet or drawer? Are you dabbling in pornography when you're alone in the hotel room on business? Let me be as pointed as I can: get rid of all of it! Do it now, before you finish this chapter. Pornography has no place in our lives. It's impossible to be involved in pornography and have a pure, satisfying sexual relationship with a spouse.

Pornography by definition obviously includes what society traditionally calls pornography, from *Playboy* to hard-core magazines, from Internet porn sites to adult movies on cable. But we must set a higher standard and also evaluate many of the magazines we buy right in our neighborhood grocery store, the novels we buy at the local bookseller, or the mainstream television shows and movies that have become more and more sexually explicit. Many of the things we read and watch may not be technically labeled as pornography, but nonetheless they can lead us down the path of lustful thoughts. Get this stuff out of your life. Don't give excuses: "I can watch this movie. It's a great movie with an excellent theme. There are a few questionable parts but I can handle them." Those questionable parts, those illicit scenes, can leave a trail of lust in your mind for months and months.

Psychologists and psychiatrists tell us our subconscious is

photographic. It doesn't forget anything we see. We can begin to compare our marriages to what we see in a scene on television or in a movie, where the actors have had plastic surgery and wear several layers of makeup. They are working on a multimillion-dollar budget and have about ten different takes to get the scene right. You can look at that and think, "You know, our marriage isn't like that. My husband [or wife] doesn't make love to me like that or look like that. I guess there's something else better out there for me." You're believing a lie if you think that. Your eyes can deceive you in so many different areas, but especially in what you take in through the entertainment world. Remember the second alarm: Your Eyes Can Lead to Your Demise.

3. If You Flirt, You'll End Up in the Dirt

Several years ago Lisa and I had dinner with a very successful couple. They were "beautiful people." I remember them telling us, "You know, we've made a lot of money. And I'll be frank with you, Ed and Lisa, the reason we've made a lot is because we both flirt around at the office for business deals, luncheons, and business trips. It really works." As Lisa and I drove home later that night, she looked at me and said, "Ed, that marriage will never last." Four months later, they buried that marriage in the relational graveyard.

Men and women, there is a *look* we give out that sends a certain message to the opposite sex. I think you know the kind of look I'm talking about. We open up those little windows of interest that get someone else's attention. We drop those little sexual hints every now and then. Adultery always begins with a little flirtation. A married man or woman does not normally wake up one morning and say, "Today, I'm going to commit adultery." No, it happens over time, slowly but surely, as those little hints and flirtations get thrown around to the coworker or neighbor. This behavior continues until one day, you find yourself over the edge, involved in an emotional or sexual affair. And before you know it your marriage, your family, your career—your whole life ends up in the dirt.

Don't go there. Flirting can lead to destruction. And don't give me that tired, worn-out excuse that it's just an innocent flirtation. Please read this carefully: *there is no such thing as an innocent flirtation!* It simply does not exist. When you find yourself wanting to flirt with someone, sound the third alarm: If You Flirt, You'll End Up in the Dirt.

4. If You Think You're Too Tall, You'd Better Get Ready to Fall

If you ever begin to think, "Oh, adultery could never happen to a spiritual giant like me," you'd better watch out. There are two times when we are most tempted sexually. The first is during times of depression when we're emotionally drained. The second is right after a spiritual high. Oftentimes we're better at anticipating weakness during those low points and can put our guards up to stave off temptation. But during those high points, we let our guards down and set ourselves up for a fall.

King David in the Bible was called a man after God's own heart. At one point in his reign, at thirty-nine years of age, he had dominated his enemies and was at the top of his career. And then it happened. In the midst of this emotional and spiritual high, he looked down from the roof of his palace to the roof of a house below and saw Bathsheba. He was probably a little bored that day. He had just seen a lot of action, and all of his men, including Bathsheba's husband, were still out on the battlefield. David, unfortunately, was not able to turn from the temptation of watching this woman bathing on her rooftop. It was common in biblical times for women to take baths on their roofs in the afternoon, because most of the men were either in battle or in the fields. Cisterns were located on the rooftops to catch rainwater, which the afternoon sun warmed.

David should have been in battle, but he wasn't. And when he took that first look at Bathsheba the temptation was just beginning to crystallize. David hadn't messed up yet. He just saw a woman. We see many members of the opposite sex who are attractive. That is not the sin. Here is where David started getting into trouble: he saw her and should have turned from the temptation. But he looked *again* and saw she was very beautiful. King David began to paint pictures in his mind of this woman and himself getting together sexually. That's when the sin began to occur in his mind. The final downfall came when he sent someone to find out about her. He began to take those fantasies from his mind and play them out. He could have stopped at any stage, at any point along the way, but he played with it. He thought about it, he focused on it. And then he did it.

David had it all. He was at the peak and pinnacle of his life. But he played the fool with sexual sin and had an affair—one that led to the murder of Bathsheba's husband and a lifetime of pain for David and Bathsheba. He thought he was too tall, but he fell. When you are at the top of your game, when you feel invincible, when you think, "I can't fall," get ready. It's time to sound the alarm, because If You Think You're Too Tall, You'd Better Get Ready to Fall.

5. Your Dress Can Lead to a Marital Mess

The way you dress can lead to a marital mess. I'm not saying we should walk around with burlap sacks on and our faces covered. We should look attractive by taking what God has given us and doing the best we can with it. But there's a way to dress tastefully and fashionably without doing so provocatively. The way some people—men and women alike—dress is like holding up a sign that says, "I'm available. I'm ready for an affair."

If you are a woman, let me say a word to you especially. Please don't think I'm picking on you, but you must be especially careful about this because of the way men are wired. Men, more than women, are visually stimulated. When men see a woman dressed a certain way, it captures their attention and leads them down the path of lust. If you don't understand how your dress can affect a man, ask your husband to share honestly what provocative dress does to him.

I don't think I need to go into details about appropriate dress. Husbands and wives, you should be aware just by the responses you get from others what does or doesn't lead others to lust after you. Again, I'm not indicating it's wrong to have a good figure, to dress well, or even to impress others with the way you look. But the question is are they impressed by you or tempted to undress you with their eyes? Admittedly, there are two sides to this coin: the person doing the dressing and the person doing the looking. One has the responsibility to dress appropriately and the other the responsibility to look at others with respect and dignity. However, if you are aware that the way you dress is tempting others, it's time to sound the fifth alarm: Your Dress Can Lead to a Marital Mess.

Parenthetically, since this is a parenting book, let me say something about how our taste for fashion as parents plays out in the way our kids dress. Our kids take their fashion cues from us. I'm not saying they dress exactly like us; most teens wouldn't be caught dead in the same clothes their parents wear. But they watch how their parents dress and evaluate whether they practice what they preach. If you aren't leading the way in this area by modeling appropriate clothing choices, you have no recourse in getting onto your kids about the way they dress. So if you want your kids, your teens, to dress better, you may need to start by giving them better cues.

6. Those Who Are Close Can Tempt You the Most

The sixth alarm is another critical safeguard against infidelity. It's the knowledge that those who are closest to you can tempt you the most. Your friends must have the same commitment to marital fidelity that you and your spouse do. I've sat behind my desk, time after time, and I've heard the same story: "Pastor, I thought he [or she] loved me, but he [she] ran off with my best friend." Here's what I've discovered over the years as I've talked with different people in marital distress. Affairs occurred most often with those who were friends of the couple. The second most likely place for them to occur was in the workplace. And the third most likely scenario, believe it or not, was an affair with an in-law.

Regarding affairs with friends, we have the most control over these relationships because we can pick the people with whom we hang out. If you regularly spend time with people who don't have the same marital commitment you and your spouse do, get out of those relationships. I know that sounds harsh, but you must do it for the sake of your marriage and family. Don't hang around, hoping their values will change. If you are feeling pulled into an affair with a friend, you need to end that relationship *now*!

Let me also address affairs in the workforce. The workplace is a prime location for infidelity. It is likely you spend more time with the people you work with than you do with your own family. If you put in forty hours a week, you're spending at least two thousand hours a year and ninety thousand hours over the course of a lifetime at work. Add in long lunches and business trips and dinners, and you're spending a lot of your waking time with your coworkers. Oftentimes a man and woman end up working together into the evening, traveling together, or having meals together. These times alone with coworkers of the opposite sex are prime invitations to infidelity.

Let me share some guidelines my wife and I have established for my work and ministry. I encourage you to develop some similar guidelines for yourself if you're in the workforce. These will help you to avoid any opportunity for sexual temptation.

- I never ride alone with a woman in a car unless it's my wife.

- I never counsel a woman alone. One or two of my assistants must be in my office and the door must remain open when I counsel a woman.

- I never go by myself to meet a woman in a public place.

- I never travel alone. I travel with either my wife or one of my male friends or associates.

These guidelines have helped me not only to avoid any sexual temptations but also to avoid any misconceptions people may have by seeing me in an inappropriate situation.

Are you being tempted by your friends, your coworkers, your spouse's relatives, or any other acquaintances? Do you feel the tug of infidelity on the sleeve of your heart? Maybe it's time to sound the sixth alarm: Those Who Are Close Can Tempt You the Most.

7. Communicate Before It's Too Late

Another way to secure our homes against infidelity is to install the Communicate Before It's Too Late alarm in our marriages. And one of the best ways my wife and I have found to communicate strategically and meaningfully is to do the Sweet Sixteen.

Let me explain. About twelve years ago I worked with a gentleman by the name of R. C. Smith. R. C. was a great guy, a very encouraging person. He came to my office regularly, and every time he talked he smiled. He always asked how I was and then told me he appreciated me. He thanked me for all the work I did and for the opportunity to work with me. I responded that the feeling was mutual. He did this almost every day.

One afternoon when we were talking, I asked him to explain to me some of the reasons that his marriage was so great. (By the way, it is helpful for young couples to have older couples, whose marriages are solid, in whom they can confide and from whom they can learn.) As a young married man, I found it tremendously helpful to speak with R. C. about the things that made his marriage successful.

The one piece of advice that stood out for me during that afternoon conversation so many years ago was something

R. C. called the Sweet Sixteen. He said he and his wife, Charlotte, practiced the Sweet Sixteen every day when he came home. When I asked for elaboration, he said they looked at each other for sixteen minutes and took turns talking and listening.

That's pretty strong advice. But to do this Sweet Sixteen the way R. C. and his wife did, you have to get away from the distractions of technology, housework, jobs, and the demands of your kids. You have to prioritize your marital relationship above everything else. Doing this exercise together right after work may not be the best time for you. That's okay. Do it in the morning, before dinner, after dinner, after the kids go to bed, or right before you go to bed—whatever works best for you. Just remember to do it when you're both alert and able to engage in meaningful conversation. If one of you is a night person and the other a morning person, neither of those times will work for you as a couple; one of you will always be too zoned out to really communicate. You need to pick a time-zone-sensitive period that works for both of you.

Lisa and I on many nights will take our Sweet Sixteen as soon as I come home from work so we can catch up on each other's day. We tell the kids that Mom and Dad need some time alone and to go outside or to their rooms and play or finish their homework. Or, as I pointed out in the first chapter, at other times we'll wait until the kids go to bed to connect. Our children know this time is important to our marriage relationship.

Obviously, the number of minutes is not the issue. The important thing is that you stake out your relational territory in your household as husband and wife and make a daily commitment to take time to communicate, to share, and to listen.

Find a regular time and place to make this happen. Many homes have sitting areas in the master bedrooms or studies that would be conducive for the Sweet Sixteen. You might need to go out on the front porch or for a walk. Do whatever works best, but make it happen.

Now most likely, if you are the wife, you're saying, "Oh, I like that." On the other hand, as a husband you just may not get this whole Sweet Sixteen concept. Guys, let me put it in our vernacular. Most of us watch sports interviews. We see or hear the TV personality thrust a microphone into an athlete's face and ask a question. Then he or she asks several follow-up questions. In other words, the reporter interviews the athlete.

Husbands, do the same with your spouse. Don't think about it as the Sweet Sixteen. Instead, think of it as an interview with your spouse. After work, ask her how her day was. Then ask her several follow-up questions. Don't just *act* as if you're listening. Dive into her world. Put yourself in her shoes.

Guys, women communicate differently from men. They talk about their feelings first, and then the facts. Because of this, you have to ask enough questions to get past the feelings so you can connect. Identify with what she's saying. Make eye contact. The Bible says the eyes are the windows of our souls. Also, pay attention to how you communicate with your body language, because your body expresses your interest more than your words do. Then summarize mentally what she's saying and repeat it back to her so you know you have connected. All of those things are huge in communication.

Now, wives, you know guys communicate first with the facts. After you wade through all of the facts, you can get to the feelings. That is just the way it is. So, wives, do the Sweet Sixteen, and husbands, the interview.

The Bible says this about communication: "Everyone should be quick to listen, slow to speak and slow to become angry" (James 1:19 NIV). Never underestimate the power of just listening in conversation. Studies indicate 7 percent of communication is done with words, 38 percent with tone, and 55 percent with facial expressions.[2] Whether these statistics are exactly accurate or not, the overall principle is evident. You can send your spouse the wrong message with the eye roll, various facial expressions, and obvious body language. When you listen, you drive the conversation—the listener does, not the talker.

One final note: when you talk, don't enter what I refer to as the Moan Zone. Too many couples just whine to each other. After a steady diet of that, you can smell the spoiled fish. We need to share the tough things, but let's not forget the good stuff, too. If you aren't regularly building and benefiting each other with positive communication, then you need to sound the seventh alarm: Communicate Before It's Too Late.

8. Creatively Date Your Mate

The eighth alarm is my favorite. And this should be your favorite alarm as well, husbands and wives: Creatively Date Your Mate. In essence, keep your marital lawn so green that all the other grass looks brown. When Lisa looks at another man, she should not think lustful thoughts about him; her marital lawn should be so green that she wouldn't even want to entertain that thought. Instead she'd be thinking, "There's no way this guy will challenge me spiritually, the way Ed does. There's no way this guy will meet my needs, physically, the way Ed does. Why trade in a Rolls-Royce for a pair of roller skates?" Our spouses should say that about us.

A couple shared with me that they had not gone on a date night in a year. An entire year had gone by without the two of them connecting one-on-one as a couple. I have to be blunt: that is a pathetic situation. This couple has two teenage sons, and they are what I would call the quintessential kid-CEO family. Everything revolves around the kids—their sports, their school, and their schedules.

How about you? Are you taking time to connect on a regular basis with your spouse? Are you keeping the romance alive by continuing to court your spouse? Do you dress up and go out a couple of times a month just so the two of you can have fun together? Do you act like teenagers in love going out on dates, to the movies, to the mall, on picnics, to a concert, or to a nice restaurant? Have you done something fun and spontaneous together lately? Have you? If not, isn't it about time you did?

The best thing you can do for kids, parents, is not related to having them in certain sports. It is not related to having them in *this* group or *that* activity. All of that stuff is fine and dandy. But the best thing is for you to give them a wonderful marriage, and the best way to have a wonderful marriage is to regularly, strategically, and creatively date your mate.

Your children watch you 24/7. How do they know about communication? How do they know about forgiveness? How do they know about love? How do they know about intimacy? They learn it all by watching the ways Mom and Dad relate to one another in marriage. As you go out together and come back with stars in your eyes and your arms around each other, they see the love, the intimacy, and the security of a home built on the foundation of a solid marriage. It is vital that you keep that connection so that they have something worthwhile to watch.

Guys, I'm going to pick on you regarding this date night thing. I believe you should take the initiative in this area. You need to plan a date night at least twice a month. You make the call to your wife and coordinate your schedules. You set up the child care. You make the plans. Show some PDA (public displays of affection) by nonsexually touching her during the date. Walk with her and not ten feet in front of her. Open the car door for her. Put her on a pedestal and show her the same kind of attention you did when you were courting.

Why am I picking on the guys? I may seem old-fashioned, but I believe men should do the same things to keep their wives as they used to get them. In other words, courtship and dating should not end with marriage. When you take the initiative in this area, you are saying to your wife, "You are still special to me and I never want to take our relationship for granted. I want to honor you by planning a regular time when we can connect." Also—I'm speaking for my own family—Lisa is the major planner and administrator in our household. And when I take on the planning of the date night, it makes that night very special for her because it does not require extra work for her. Depending on the unique roles and responsibilities in your relationship, it might work better for you and your spouse to take turns planning the date night. That's great. Do whatever works for you, but just make it happen on a regular basis.

As an aside to marital dating, let me address any single mothers who are reading this: single ladies, when you date, the guy should open car doors, he should defer to you, he should plan the date, and he should be creative. If he does not do these things, head for the hills, get out of town, leave him. Life is too short to date a loser. If he does not date you creatively or treat you with respect, with courtesy, and with deference, he is a loser in my book. And to be fair, the same could be said for men dating rude, disrespectful women.

A lot of women say, "Well, once they throw rice on our heads, *then* it will be romance and marital bliss." Trust me: it won't. He will not be miraculously transformed into Prince Charming, so you better watch him now. That's why the courtship and dating period is so important.

Let me get back to the married couples. I promise you, if you will make a commitment to have a date night at least twice a month, you will not believe what will happen in your marriage. Lisa and I have a date night every Thursday, and it's like an oasis in the middle of the week. It's something we look forward to more than anything else. And the only time we miss it is if someone is sick or something unforeseeable happens to change our plans.

If going out with your spouse doesn't excite you more than anything else you do, you need to begin now to reestablish that connection and rekindle the flame that was sparked during the courtship years. And if the date night is not a part of your family security system against infidelity, you need to install the eighth alarm: Creatively Date Your Mate.

So how about it? How does your home measure up? Is the sanctity of your marriage and family securely protected by an eight-alarm security system? If not, it's time to do a security screening and assess your vulnerabilities. I would strongly encourage you to work together in your marriage to hold each other accountable in these eight critical areas: making unfair comparisons, flirting, lust, spiritual pride, dress, friendships, communication, and dating.

Plan an Affair with Your Spouse

There is one final thing I would like to suggest to help you affair-proof your marriage, and that is to make your marriage a lifelong love affair. Let me explain.

In his book *Acres of Diamonds*, author Russell H. Conwell recounted this classic story: Ali Hopkins, a very wealthy man, lived in Persia. One day, a wise man walked up on his property and said, "Ali, if you could only own diamonds, if you could only have a diamond mine, you could own anything in the world." Hopkins thought about it for a while. He began to rack his brain. He finally sold all of his estate, all of his property, and all of his orchards. He left his wife and family with some friends, and he went in search of some diamonds.

He traveled extensively to Palestine and Europe. But he didn't find his diamond mine. Years went by. He spent all of his money in search of diamonds only to end up standing on the coast of Barcelona, Spain, in rags—a dying man. While he stood on that lonely beach, a giant wave rolled in and Hopkins threw himself into the sea, never to be seen again.

Back in Persia, the farmer who'd purchased Ali Hopkins's land was leading his camel to a small brook that ran right by Ali's house. As the camel came up to the brook, stuck out its giant tongue, and began lapping the water, the gentleman who purchased the land looked down and saw something shiny. He began to move some of the dirt, rocks, and sediment around to see what had caught his eye. It was a diamond! That farmer discovered the largest diamond mine in the history of the world right there on Ali Hopkins's property—the Kimberly Diamond Mine, which has produced the largest crown jewels in the world.

What's the point? What's the principle? Ali Hopkins was standing on acres and acres of diamonds right in his own backyard, but he missed out on that wealth by trying to find diamonds in someone else's backyard, only to end up in utter ruin.

Husband, wife, instead of looking for diamonds in someone else's yard and having an affair, maybe it's time to plan an affair with your own spouse. You're standing on acres and acres of diamonds in your marriage. Move some of the rock and sediment around, discover the wealth you have, and begin to mine those diamonds. That's what God wants us to do. That is how we can protect our marital mansion from the devastation of infidelity.

Be a security guard. Install that eight-alarm security system around your marital mansion, and continue a lifelong love affair with your spouse. That is what God wants for your life and mine. Don't ever say you're above temptation, because temptation is no respecter of persons. Build that marital mansion and one day you'll look around and find yourself staring at countless diamonds in your own backyard.

{ 6 }

Sex Busters and Builders

BEFORE WE DIVE INTO this next chapter, let me explain why I'm addressing sexual issues in a book on parenting. I feel that I've already established the importance of marriage in the family system. Marriage is a key element in maintaining the strength of the family. And likewise sexual intimacy is a key element in maintaining the strength of the marriage. That's why it's called a family *system*. Every component is critical. Every part is significant. You cannot put your sex life in a box and pretend it doesn't affect the entire family.

Sex is one of the most intimate ways we have to connect with our spouses. And working hard to maintain that connection communicates the priority of marriage in the home. Remember the flow chart: God, marriage, kids. The strength of that connection also spills over into the way we connect with our children. Your sex life in marriage can either spread a ray of sunshine in your home or cast an ominous shadow. When that intimate part of your marital life is flourishing, your kids know it. They may not understand what sex is but they know when Mommy and Daddy are connecting and when they're not.

Just so you know from the outset, I'm not going to be talking a lot about children in this chapter. Marriage is second on the family flow chart and so this chapter is going to focus on that priority. This is for you, Mom and Dad. This is time to focus on your marriage relationship—specifically on the key ingredient of sexual intimacy. So, with that in mind, let's find out how to replace those sex busters in marriage with sex builders.

God-Given Desire

One morning several years ago, one of my twin daughters, who was five at the time, looked up at me and said, "Dad, when you saw Mommy for the first time, did you whistle?"

I thought for a moment about our teenage years and the first time I saw Lisa, and then I answered, "Yes, I'm sure I did." I was a red-blooded American teenage boy with raging hormones. Lisa was (and still is, might I add) a very beautiful woman, and I was physically attracted to her.

God gives us that wolf-whistle desire for the opposite sex. He gives us the gift of sex and has provided a powerful place, a valuable venue, to practice and to utilize that gift. I'm referring, of course, to the marriage bed.

Lisa and I were obviously attracted to one another sexually before we were married, but we saved ourselves for marriage. And we can honestly say now, after twenty years and the addition of four kids into our lives, we have worked hard to maintain a mutually satisfying sexual relationship. We realize, however, that not all married couples—especially those with children—share our experience. In fact, adding kids into the mix of marriage often serves to increase sexual tension and dissatisfaction. Thus, we are confronted with an important question in this section on intimacy: how do we maintain a vibrant, exciting sex life during the parenting years?

You're probably not accustomed to seeing the two phrases "parenting years" and "exciting sex life" in the same sentence. I suspect that for many parents those phrases appear to be mutually exclusive. Contrary to popular opinion on the matter, I submit to you that marriage can be a place of incredible sexual fulfillment—before, during, and after the parenting years. But there are some obstacles or barriers we must overcome in order to achieve this kind of sexual satisfaction.

With that in mind, throughout this chapter, we will be taking a look at some Sex Busters in marriage. You may be thinking, "Sex Busters? That's kind of a negative spin on sex, isn't it? I thought this was going to be about Sex Builders." And you are right. Normally, I don't like to present the negative side of principles. But in this case I decided to contrast several negative Sex Busters with an equal number of positive Sex Builders.

Sex is a good thing. It is from God, and he wants us to experience great sex. However, it's no secret that couples experience various levels of sexual frustration, especially during the parenting years. Ask just about anyone with children and they will tell you this is a reality in their lives. And I suspect it is a reality in your life as well to one degree or another. What causes this frustration? What are the hang-ups that serve as Sex Busters? Sex Busters are attitudes or habits that keep us from using this God-given gift in a God-ordained way. On the flip side of each Sex Buster is a Sex Builder. Sex Builders will help you get rid of the things that keep you from being the kind of mate, sexually speaking, that God wants you to be. If you want to make love regularly and creatively, you had better deal with this subject matter.

Whenever I speak in church on the subject of sex, I'm amazed at how people pay attention. No one sleeps. No one drifts off into daydreams. No one counts ceiling lights. Some people think we should not talk in the church about sex. Whoever thinks that, though, doesn't know the Bible.

We should not be ashamed to talk about what God was not ashamed to create and to put in print. The two most prominent places where we should discuss this matter are the home and the church. Historically, the church has done a pathetic job in talking about sex. Thankfully, some churches are trying to change that by getting real and searching for what the Bible says about this subject.

And, as I always say when I'm speaking on the subject of sex, listen up, singles. If you are a single parent, pay attention to these sex busters and builders. You may not be dealing with these issues at this particular point in your life, but you may in the not too distant future.

Sex Buster #1:
You Don't Know What God Says about Sex

When couples are unaware of God's take on the subject, unaware of what the Bible says, they are facing a Sex Buster. If you don't have the biblical knowledge, information, and application principles regarding this subject, you cannot have the kind of great sex life that will bond you and your spouse like superglue. Gary Chapman wrote this about the sexual experience in marriage in his book *Covenant Marriage*: "No other human experience is more intimate than the sexual experience. It celebrates our emotional, intellectual, and spiritual intimacy. It is a bonding experience."[1] This is so critical for parents, because our sexual relationship and connection as a couple will provide a foundation for unity in parenting.

Yet most couples are unaware of what the Bible says about frequency, about when one person is in the mood and the other is not, about romance, and about being innovative in the bedroom.

Sex Builder #1: Get in Sync with Scripture

When you don't know or understand what God says about something, find out. The Sex Builder is that we have to get in sync with scriptural sexuality—what the Bible has to say about the gift of sex within the context of marriage. There is a huge link between spirituality and sexuality. Couples who make time to express love to God in an authentic way make time to make love regularly.

I have talked to numerous couples who have wonderfully, mutually satisfying sexual relationships in marriage. And I have observed that the most sexually satisfied people in marriage are those who pray together, those who read the Bible together, and those who go to church together. God made sex and they are doing sex the way he wants them to do it.

One of the foundational passages from the Bible regarding God's agenda for sexuality in marriage is 1 Corinthians 7:3–5. It reads, "The husband should not deprive his wife of sexual intimacy, which is her right as a married woman, nor should the wife deprive her husband. The wife gives authority over her body to her husband, and the husband also gives authority over his body to his wife. So do not deprive each other of sexual relations."

These verses address management, don't they? Your spouse is in management over your body. He is. She is. You're thinking, "You are kidding me, Ed!" Look at the passage one more time: "The wife gives authority over her body to her husband, and the husband also gives authority over his body to his wife." Are you in sync with Scripture? Or are you playing games with your spouse? Has sex become a bargaining chip of manipulation and control? That's not the way God intended us to use it. God has given sex as a gift to be shared, lovingly and willingly, with our spouses. When a husband and wife get in sync with this, they give the management of their bodies wholly and completely to the other.

Sex Buster #2:
You Don't Understand Your Spouse's Sex Drive

Men and women are different. What a profound statement, right? It may seem obvious, but in this age of unisex everything, some couples are clueless about the difference between men's and women's sex drives.

Let's look at the man's drive. A man's sex drive is kind of like a sprint. In an instant, just like that, he's ready to race into sex. He can get sexually excited in a moment's time, and immediately he is ready to go. A woman's sex drive, on the other hand, is more like a 5K run. She more or less jogs into sex. God has wired us differently, and we have unique sex drives. A husband experiences sex, and from sex flow the feelings. The wife, on the other hand, has to experience feelings, and from there flows the sex.

Here, though, are the problems that occur with these differing sex drives. The husband, the sprinter, approaches his wife the way he wants to be approached—with immediate sexual stimulation and gratification. Being more aggressive and taking the initiative, he sprints into sex.

What does the wife do? She approaches her husband the way she wants to be approached—with romance, with intimacy, with gentleness. She jogs into sex. So you've got a problem and some sexual tension going on. You have one party doing his thing his way and the other party doing her thing her way. As the famous, now retired, football commentator used to say, "Whoa, Nelly."

Sex Builder #2: Discover the Pace of Passion

Since so many of us are clueless about the varying sex drives in men and women, what do we do? What is the Sex Builder? Wives and husbands who have it together on the sexual front are able to find a mutually satisfying pace of passion.

Let me talk to the men first. For the most part, we desire sex more than our wives do—not all the time, not across the board, but in most situations and circumstances. Most of us men are keenly aware of what it's like when we make our move and she doesn't like the move or she is not in the mood. We know the rejection we feel when that occurs. If you're a man, you know exactly what I'm talking about.

In his book *Give and Take: The Secret to Marital Compatibility,* Christian psychologist Dr. Willard F. Harley Jr. gave an eye-opening illustration regarding a man's sex drive. I believe it really helps women identify with a man's sex drive and appreciate what a man goes through when she rejects him. Imagine, first of all, a stool with a glass of water sitting on it. The husband is next to the stool and the wife is next to him. The wife is immobilized. She can't get to the water. The husband is the only one who can get the water for her.

Here's what happens. The wife turns to her husband and asks, "Honey, would you please pour me a glass of water? I'm getting thirsty."

The husband turns and responds, "I don't really feel like it. I'm not in the mood. Maybe in a couple of hours."

Hours roll by. One more time the wife turns to her husband. "Honey, I'm getting thirsty. Would you please give me a glass of water?"

The husband responds, "You know, I'm kind of tired. I've had a long day, okay?"

Then the wife begins to get angry. She can feel her temperature rising. She is craving a glass of water at this point, so she begins to demand it: "I want a glass of water! You're the only one who can give me the glass of water!"

The husband looks at his wife, spins on his heels, and says, "You're not going to get any water with an attitude like that."

The husband returns to the scene about a day later, and the wife is livid. Finally, the husband says, "Okay. Here's your water. Just drink it!"

When the wife is gulping down the water, do you think she's satisfied? Do you think her thirst is really quenched? Not really. She's thinking she is going to be thirsty again, and if she wants another drink, she had better watch what she says to her husband.[2]

So goes a man's sex drive. As water quenches his thirst physically, sex in marriage quenches his thirst in a physical, spiritual, emotional, and psychological manner. But sex must be
given and received with the right spirit if it is to truly satisfy
those longings.

Well, now let's pick on the men. Men are so compartmentalized, so structured, that most of us are brainless concerning
the overall context of the relationship and how that affects the
sexual connection. We are, for the most part, one-dimensional
people.

While boarding an airplane not too long ago, I walked by a
group of women. One of the women was reading a book entitled *All About Men.* I stopped and asked, "All about men?"

She said, "Yeah, it's a short book."

I nearly died laughing. I took my seat about ten rows back
and thought, "I'm going to put that in one of my books."

The house could be dirty. You could have just been in a
major argument five minutes earlier. You may have just had to
deal with work or kids or any of a number of tiring things. If
you're a man, though, you're still likely to pat your wife on the
posterior and say, "Hey, hey, hey! How about now?"

Wives, on the other hand, are multifaceted and multidimensional. The context surrounding the sexual part of the
relationship is huge for them. They have to know that everything is A-OK outside the master bedroom before everything
gets A-OK between the sheets.

So what do we do about it? Yes, there are those times when
the husband and wife are both in the mood, when they both
want to make love. But what do you do when one is ready for
it and the other is not?

Husband, here is what you do: you slow down. Quit being a

sprinter all the time, and jog a little bit. It's sometimes fun to jog. Wife, don't always run so slowly. Try incorporating some sprints into that 5K. When the husband is thinking about her needs and the wife is thinking about his needs, when the husband is doing some jogging and the wife some sprinting, you have two people discovering the pace of passion. If you want to get your partner in the mood, approach him or her the way he or she wants to be approached.

Sex Buster #3:
You Have Unrealistic Ideas about Sex

Because of misleading portrayals of sex in novels, TV, movies, popular music, and other media, many couples have unrealistic expectations regarding sex in their real-life relationships.

When I was at Florida State University, a good friend of mine and I watched movies together every once in a while. Every time he saw something that was lame, that was a reach, he said, "Ehhhhh, unrealistic." The first couple of times it was funny, but after the tenth time I wanted to hit him.

But he was right. Like my friend, we need to identify—perhaps in a less annoying way—unrealistic ideas and images regarding sexuality every time we see and hear them. Because virtually everywhere we turn, in every avenue of life, we get hit with this stuff over and over again.

Taking our popular, modern-day romantic comedies as an example, sex rarely, if ever, happens the way it does on the silver screen. For one thing, as I indicated in chapter 4, the vast majority of sexual references in popular entertainment are outside the marriage bed. In these shows and movies, a man and a woman just look at each other, and five seconds later they rip off their clothes. That's not the way it happens in marriage. In their book *Great Sexpectations*, Dr. Robert and Rosemary Barnes observed, "Many movies today have cranked it up a notch. Moving quickly through the romantic interaction, if there is any at all, the relationship instantly becomes sexual."[3] When you see stuff like this in movies, you need to just say, "Ehhhhh, unrealistic." Better yet, don't watch movies and television shows that portray such an unrealistic and, might I add, ungodly picture of sex.

If the Hollywood crowd had it down cold, their lives wouldn't be so messed up. If you had to be buff and beautiful to have great sex, then they would have a corner on the market. But we're talking about some unhappy people. All you have to do is go through the checkout line at the grocery store and look at the front covers of the magazines to see that these people's lives score pretty low on the relational scale. Don't measure your sexuality through the grid of the movies, the videos, and the secular media. That's not the real story.

Let me also address pornography in the bedroom at this point. It has become somewhat in vogue these days to bring adult videos into the bedroom. Husbands and wives rationalize this by saying that it will give them a sexual boost to watch another couple make love: "What turns them on turns us on." I have read the research. Don't go there.

First of all, when you bring an adult video into the bedroom, you're involved in lusting after and being aroused by another person or persons. The excuse that you're just watching and not actually involved with someone else does not hold biblical water. Christ said that if you lust after someone in your heart, then you are committing adultery.

Second of all, pornography will always make you want more and more. You will get addicted to the extra stimulation and will start to need it just to be aroused with your spouse.

Here's some straightforward advice: if you are involved with pornographic videos, throw them out and don't get another one. And by all means, if you have reached the level of addiction, get help from a good Christian counselor or support group. Addiction to pornography, if you do not deal with it seriously and swiftly, has the potential to leave an otherwise good marriage on the ash heap. Do whatever it takes, now, to remove this incendiary influence from your life—before it's too late.

Sex Builder #3:
See Through the Secular Smoke Screen

See through the secular smoke screen that distorts the realities of a biblical commitment in marriage. Run your love life through the God Grid (more on that in chapter 8) and see what the Bible says about one man and one woman committed to God and to each other in the context of marriage—a man and woman who are selfless, who are serving, who are creative, who make love and see sex as a part of mutual discipleship.

I devoted an entire chapter in this book to the harmful cultural influences that are slamming against the walls of the home and threatening the minds and hearts of our children. These same influences are pounding away at our marriages and can derail them if we are not careful. Don't get your ideas of love and sex from TV, movies, music, the arts, or any other form of mass media. Get your ideas instead from the Author and Creator of human sexuality—God himself. Only he can help you see through the smoke screen and experience the pure joy of sex the way he meant it to be.

Sex Buster #4: You've Lost the Look

This Sex Buster is such an obvious issue and yet something we often overlook. Men, in particular, after we're married, say, "Hey, I've got my spouse. I can lose the look and gain the weight. I don't have to look good anymore. You should have seen me when I was dating her, though! Boy, I knew what to do then."

Some men are so pitiful at this physical appearance stuff that they still walk around with that high school jock look, complete with the same old gym shorts, tattered tank top, and rough, unshaven face. They're thinking, "Hey, baby, I've still got it, you know." The wives are wondering why they should even want to *touch* them.

Here is what the wives do: they end up wearing one of those "Not tonight, honey" nightgowns to bed. You know what I'm talking about—the kind that screams "Headache!"

We can laugh at these humorous scenarios, but they represent a real-life problem in many marriages. After we say "I do," we often follow it up with "I don't." We think, "I don't need to work hard to look good for my spouse anymore." "I don't need to worry about competing for her or dating her." "I don't have to impress him any longer by taking care of my body."

Being a pastor is something I absolutely love. There is nothing like it. I see the good. I see the miracles of God as I witness lives being changed regularly. But I also see the other side. I see the results of sin and the devastation of relationships that go astray. What often amazes me, though, is the physical transformation of someone who is recently separated, divorced, or involved in an extramarital affair.

Maybe a man who's involved in adultery will come and talk to me about it. I'll look at him and think, "What happened to you? You lost twenty-five pounds. You're dressing cool and have a different hairstyle. You're working for it now with this other person. Why didn't you work for it in your marriage?"

I'll see a woman who has just gone through a divorce. She has lost forty pounds and looks as if she just had a total makeover. Why didn't she do it when she was married?

While there are some exceptions—this is by no means something that happens across the board—I have to ask again, "Why?"

On the way to the airport one time, I spotted a sign that said, "It's all about work." That should be your marital bumper sticker. One of the things I've noticed about great marriages is that they maintain a tireless MWE: a Marital Work Ethic. The sad thing is that we're all weaned on the words of our culture. If it is not quick, easy, express, overnight, or disposable, then we assume somehow it's not that good, it doesn't really work, and it can't be gratifying.

Then one day we get married and discover marriage takes work, negotiation, sweat, toil, pain, and sacrifice—and that it is for keeps. Our disposable culture clashes with the permanency of the marriage relationship. No wonder so many marriages today don't make it.

Ask God to develop within your spirit a tireless Marital Work Ethic. It takes work to deal with all of these Sex Busters, but it especially takes a commitment of hard work to continue to court your spouse by maintaining your physical appearance. Don't neglect the obvious: you can't keep your sex life in shape if you don't keep yourself in shape.

Sex Builder #4: Take Care of the Temple

This Sex Builder comes from 1 Corinthians 6:19–20: "Don't you know that your body is the temple of the Holy Spirit, who lives in you and was given to you by God? You do not belong to yourself, for God bought you with a high price. So you must honor God with your body." Take care of the temple. If you are a Christ-follower, your body is a temple, the dwelling place of the Holy Spirit of God.

We have a saying in my home state: "Don't mess with Texas." Well, God is saying, "Don't trash the temple." I'm not talking about turning into a Ken and Barbie–type couple with a physical obsession that takes over your lives. I am saying, though, to do the best you can with what you have.

Eating properly, working out, and staying as lean as possible are acts of worship to God. The Bible also says in Romans 12:1 to "give your bodies to God. Let them be a living and holy sacrifice." It is an act of love for your spouse and for God when you take care of this temple called the human body.

Sex Buster #5:
You Are Making Excuses Instead of Making Love

Sex Buster #5 is the "great refusal." You know what I'm talking about. One wants it, the other says, "No, I'm tired. I'm fatigued. That's all you think about." This is different from Sex

Buster #2 which addressed how your spouse's sex drive may physically and psychologically differ from your own and how you can discover a mutual pace of passion. What I'm addressing in this section is the spiritual implication of depriving one another sexually.

Let me share with you what happens when you respond negatively to your spouse's advances. First of all, you can shame your spouse by your response. By constantly turning your spouse down, you are communicating that something must be wrong with his or her desires or that his or her needs are not legitimate. Furthermore, it takes a certain amount of vulnerability to ask someone to meet your sexual needs, and it's embarrassing and defeating when your spouse rejects you.

Second, you can mess up your relationship with God. It is a sin to ignore your spouse's sexual needs, and any sin puts a strain on your connection with God. Over and over again, the Bible compares the marriage relationship with the relationship that Jesus Christ has with the church. Because of this unique correlation, when your marriage relationship is strained, you are a poor reflection of that spiritual connection.

Third, you are inviting heightened temptations for both you and your spouse. Sadly, when husbands and wives do not get what they need at home, they often go looking elsewhere for it. From adultery to divorce, the potentially devastating results of this kind of wandering eye are obvious.

Sex Builder #5: Stop Depriving One Another

Don't make excuses. Make love. Believe it or not, that is actually a paraphrase from the Bible. Yes, the Bible actually addresses the situation where one spouse is in the mood and the other is not. They were actually having arguments about that back in biblical times, and the Book of 1 Corinthians deals with the issue.

We see it clearly in 1 Corinthians 7:5: "So do not deprive each other of sexual relations. The only exception to this rule would be the agreement of both husband and wife to refrain from sexual intimacy for a limited time, so they can give themselves more completely to prayer." Aside from certain medical problems or health issues, the only excuse we should give is, "I'm in prayer." But you must both agree.

While studying this issue, I spoke with one of the other pastors on our staff to get his input. This was his take on the subject: "Yeah, if the husband and wife do agree to abstain for a while, I know what the husband will be praying for: sex!"

All kidding aside, the verse in 1 Corinthians continues, "Afterward they should come together again so that Satan won't be able to tempt them because of their lack of self-control." I don't think the Bible tells us never to say no. But no should be the exception. And don't just say no; make an appointment: "No, but how about in a couple of hours?" or "No, but can we make a date for tomorrow morning or tomorrow night?"

A big excuse these days is "I'm tired." But being fatigued is, for the most part, a mental thing. I love to fish and especially to fly-fish in salt water. When I'm on a fishing trip, I can get up at 4 A.M., ready to go. I might be physically tired, but mentally I'm ready to fly-fish for tarpon. And that mental attitude helps refresh my body.

Are you too tired for sex—even twenty, thirty, forty-five minutes with your partner? Tell yourself, "I am having sexual intercourse with my covenant partner." Say to yourself, "I am ready."

Here's a hypothetical scenario. The husband and wife are in bed and she is too tired for sex. Suddenly, the phone rings. It's her college roommate. She is transformed in the blink of an eye from a fatigued female into a fantastic conversationalist. "Hi, girlfriend! It is so great to talk to you." Her husband is thinking, "What is up with that?"

It takes two to tango. If you want great conversation, you had both better be involved in it. If you want great romance, you had both better be taking part in it. If you want great sex, you had both better be aroused, mentally and physically.

"Well, Ed, are you telling me that I have to say yes a lot?" Yes, I am. That's what the Bible says. And I am not talking about an apathetic yes: "Okay, go ahead. We can do it right now if you really want to." That is no way to have sex, let alone great sex.

Just in case you're concerned at this point that I might be biased about this issue because I'm a man, let me share something that might help change your mind. My wife, Lisa, reviewed this material and she agrees wholeheartedly with this principle. Lisa and I both understand it is our responsibility before God to fulfill each other's sexual needs. If you want to experience an incredible sex life within an incredible marriage, you must understand that it is wrong to deprive your spouse sexually.

Sex Buster #6:
You Are Letting Your Kids Block Marital Intimacy

This Sex Buster can be summarized in one word: kids. Now, children are gifts from God, but kids can and will bust up your sex life. In chapter 2 we addressed the need to establish a parent-CEO family. This is especially important as you consider how to make marital intimacy a priority in your household.

In addition to Knowledge, Intimacy, Discipline, and Structure, KIDS can also stand for Keeping Intimacy at a Distance Successfully. If you aren't having a regular date night, this Sex Buster can rear its ugly head. If you don't have regular and enforced bedtimes for the children and certain areas of the house that are off-limits during certain hours, your intimate encounters will be few and far between.

I must at this point address the issue of kids' sleeping in the same bed with their parents. Talk about a Sex Buster! One couple we know has allowed their kids to sleep in bed with them since they were born. The kids are now school age, and they still wander into their parents' bedroom in the evening to hunker down for the night. One day we actually asked this couple, "How do you find the time or place to have sex when your kids are sleeping in the same bed with you?" The wife said, "Oh, we manage to squeeze it in once a month or so. Sometimes we go into the closet and do it."

What? Are you kidding me? This is a recipe for disaster. It's bad for the kids and bad for the parents. Regardless of what you might hear from permissive parenting persuaders, virtually no good thing can come from kids' sleeping in the parents' bedroom.

Parents, if your children have formed a habit of sleeping with you, in your bed or in the same bedroom, you need to break that habit. Psychologists tell us that it takes twenty-one days to break a bad habit. So start today, and in less than a month you and your children will be free. Do whatever it takes, because the welfare of your marriage is at stake. It's going to be a battle. There's no doubt about that. It's the battle that should have been fought when your children were infants. They are going to cry and whine and complain and throw all kinds of fits, but one day the crying will stop and they will sleep through the night in their own beds. This is all part of the process of teaching and training your children to leave the home.

A parent-CEO household maintains strong boundaries around the master suite. Your bedroom should be a place for you, as husband and wife, to connect emotionally, relationally, sexually, and conversationally. If your kids invade that space, that important connection with your spouse will not happen. But the choice is up to you as the leaders of the household.

Check out the way Dr. Robert and Rosemary Barnes phrased this caution: "A child must not be allowed to interfere with her parents' sexual relationship."[4] Did you catch the word "allowed" in that quotation? Don't blame your children if your sex life is lacking. If they're interfering, it's because you have *allowed* them to. Gary Chapman wrote, "Though children get blamed for the parents' withdrawal from the marital bed, it is the couple's responsibility to find a way to have privacy so they can share life sexually."[5]

You as the leaders need to set the expectations to ensure you have regular, meaningful time together as husband and wife.

Sex Builder #6: Take a Romantic Getaway

Aside from scheduling your regular date nights, setting a consistent bedtime, and not allowing your kids to sleep with you, another way to keep your kids from blocking marital intimacy is to get on board a B-52. B stands for a "break," and 52 stands for "fifty-two weeks out of the year." Husbands and wives, I challenge you to take two trips a year aboard the B-52. Take two breaks during those fifty-two weeks in which the two of you, *without your kids,* go on a romantic getaway. Go away for love. Go away for intimacy. Go away for sex.

"Ed, you just don't know our finances. We can't afford that." Yes, you can afford it. In fact, you can't afford not to. It is better to pay the price now, and take out a loan if you have to, than to end up relationally bankrupt down the road. You don't want to neglect the B-52 only to find one day your marriage covenant carpet bombed and destroyed. Taking these breaks is worth it and will reap huge benefits in your marriage.

Sex Buster #7: You Are Sharing Sacred Stuff with the Wrong People

Okay, this one's short and sweet: do not share tidbits regarding what goes on in the bedroom with your golfing buddies, your tennis gal pals, with the person next to you at work. Don't go there.

Pay attention to the words of Hebrews 13:4: "Marriage should be honored by all, and the marriage bed kept pure" (NIV). Talking with a trusted Christian counselor or pastoral counselor is one thing, but that's where it needs to stop. If you blab this sacred stuff, your spouse will lose trust in you, and you may fan the flames of adultery.

Sex Builder #7: Discuss Sex Openly with Your Spouse

The person you should be having a sex talk with is your spouse. Sit down and share your likes and dislikes, wants and desires, problems and needs. Put them on the table and deal with them. Maybe you need to go through a book on sex such as *Restoring the Pleasure* by Drs. Cliff and Joyce Penner. You could read aloud one chapter a night together, or read it separately and highlight your favorite passages to discuss later. You won't believe what will happen when you begin to share openly and honestly with each other about your sexual needs and desires.

If you're uncomfortable talking about sexual matters, then start slowly. Keep talking until you develop a mutual comfort level for heart-to-heart sharing. Eighty-six percent of those who divorce say that the main problem was deficient communication.[6] The greatest thing in sex is communication, so you need to find a way to bring that habit into the marriage bed.

Sex Buster #8 (For Single Parents): You Are Dabbling in Premarital Sex

I've studied many of the major world religions over the years. One thing I've found in each of them, without exception, is a clear teaching against premarital sex. The downside to casual sex is so obvious and damaging that the collective wisdom of all faiths agrees on this point.

Regardless of what other belief systems say, if you are a Christian single engaging in sex outside of marriage, you are committing cosmic treason before God. I don't care if it is with your spouse-to-be or someone you have known for a long time. If you're living together and are sexually involved, you are sinning before God.

When you continue to live in sin, God *cannot* and *will not* bless any future sexual life in marriage the way he wants. I understand the temptation and allurement. We convince ourselves that it's no big deal, that it's only a physical thing and won't impact our future relationship. Premarital sex, though, is not just a casual or physical thing. It is a multifaceted and multidimensional part of the total relationship. There are spiritual, psychological, and emotional aspects to it.

When you involve yourself in premarital sex, you have a great chance of marrying the wrong person. Why? Sex is so powerful that it can hinder your reasoning abilities. You will hook up with him or her and later say, "Why in the world did I do that?" It was probably because you had intercourse with him or her.

If you are having sex now outside of marriage, stop. *Stop.* Say that you are going to unwrap the greatest gift possible for your spouse on your wedding night: your sexuality. Don't lie to yourself. God ordained sex for the marriage bed for a reason, and we need to respect the fact that, despite what we might feel, God has our best interests at heart.

I have a close friend who lives on the West Coast. He was a college athlete, and during that time he was very promiscuous. He became a Christian later on and got married.

After several years, his marriage went through some horrible problems and was hanging by a thread. He was getting ready to do something so stupid I could not believe it. Just by the grace of God and through the loving confrontations of friends, he and his wife sought counseling rather than split up. They got back on track and are now doing great. But he would be the first to tell you the reason he had those issues was because he was so promiscuous before marriage. He, so to speak, brought *all* of those girls into the bedroom.

Don't do it. It is not worth it. I know it seems like fun for a while, because oftentimes sin is fun at first. But sin not only has kicks, it has kickbacks. And the kickbacks are brutal.

Sex Builder #8: Keep Yourself Pure

This point is pretty self-explanatory. If you've messed up in the past or are in the process of messing up and messing around, stop now and save yourself for your spouse.

If you've been disciplined enough so far to keep from pre-marital sex, don't give up. I know it's hard. The temptation seems unbearable at times, but God will reward you for your faithfulness. Do whatever it takes to preserve this sacred act and reserve it for marriage.

Avoid tempting places and situations, like being alone to-gether in your apartment. Consider some group activities where you have accountability in numbers. And follow the biblical advice: "Run away from sexual sin!" (1 Cor. 6:18). When you're tempted to give in to those urges, run. Get out of there. Don't delude yourself by saying, "Oh, I can handle it." God knows this area is hard for us, so he tells us to get out be-fore the fire gets too hot.

Sex Buster #9: You Are Stuck in Monotony

You've heard about a monogamous relationship, right? That's a good thing. Well, there's something out there called a *monot-onous marriage* that is not such a good thing. In fact, it's a big-time Sex Buster. This marriage consists of the same old, same old, rutlike relationship. You've got the same old look; you're wearing the same old wardrobe, talking the same old talk, stuck in the same old place, and engaged in the same old love-making.

Instead of becoming monotonous, we need to model our lives and relationships after the person of God. God is not stuck in a rut. He is highly creative and innovative. If we know him, live for him, and worship him corporately and individually, we are going to be creative in every area of our lives.

You can't do the same things the same way and expect unique results. We have to change. We have to work. We have to kick monotony out and do sex the way God wants us to.

Sex Builder #9: Keep the Romance Alive

This Sex Builder is especially for men: keep the romance alive in your married relationship. You might be thinking, "There Ed goes again, harping about dating my spouse." I wrote in the previous chapter that the date night was one of the key ingredients to the great marriage that Lisa and I have, and I meant it. Don't forget the power of those regular times alone—again, I recommend at least twice a month to rejuvenate and keep your marriage going strong. Men, carve time out of your schedule, make it a high priority, to court your wife.

But keeping the romance alive means more than just planning dates. From the kitchen to the garage to the bedroom and back again, reigniting the romance in your marriage is an all-encompassing proposition. It's going to take some creative thinking and planning to court your spouse continually. Jerry Jenkins tackled the challenge of maintaining this courtship in his book *Loving Your Marriage Enough to Protect It*. He wrote that there is a difference in the ways that men and women feel, act, and portray their passion for each other: "The problem with ego needs and the need for romance, especially in a woman's life, is that there are hidden, unseen factors that men need to take into consideration when [relating] to [their wives]."[7] What I believe Jenkins was getting at is that it takes hard work, men, to think creatively and meet the sometimes mysterious needs of women.

Being romantically attentive to our wives means we will meet their needs for passion differently from the way we like our needs to be met. It doesn't mean we are ever going to be able to think like women think. We are not women. There is no way I am ever going to think, act, and feel the way Lisa does, and there is no way she is ever going to think, act, and feel the way I do. We are *opposite* sexes!

I like what Dr. Phil McGraw once said on his show about romancing his wife: "If I decided to get romantic and drop rose petals from my front door all the way to my bedroom and my wife, Robin, walked into the house, do you know what she would say to me? She would say, 'Phil, who is going to pick those rose petals up?'"

That's greatness right there! That's exactly right. Sometimes rose petals are nice, but you don't have to go to that extreme to be romantic. Guys, do you know what romance is? Romance is when the trash is piled up and before she says, "Would you take the trash out?" you take the trash out. It's about being attentive to the entire context of the relationship. Romance is saying kind words that build her up and make her feel beautiful. Romance is listening as she thinks out loud and shares her feelings. Romance is entering her world. Romance is doing those little things that we so often overlook.

It means rearranging our schedules to go out on dates, sending flowers and other gifts when she least expects them, and talking with her in more than one-syllable grunts. Husband, if you start doing things like that, then your entire marriage relationship will be like the first time you laid eyes on your wife. Let me say it again: what you used to get her is what you need to use to keep her.

If you look up the word *impractical* in the dictionary, one of the synonyms is *romantic*. Don't you like that? My challenge to you and your spouse is to become people of romance, in both practical and impractical ways.

When I opened this chapter, I wrote that we rarely think of the phrases "exciting sex life" and "parenting years" being in the same sentence. It is my prayer that from now on you will not think about those as mutually exclusive terms but as mutually compatible terms. You can if you will honor God and experience sex within his parameters, by using this gift the way he desires. Thank God for that wolf-whistle desire for the opposite sex, and deal with those Sex Busters by implementing Sex Builders in your marriage. When you do, I believe it will have towering implications for your entire family. You will be sending signals as a parent CEO that your marriage is vibrant and flourishing and in turn that the family flow chart is functioning as it should.

PART FOUR

Discipline

Maintaining a
Training Ground of
Loving Correction

{ 7 }

The 411 on Discipline

KIDS THESE DAYS—talk about out of control! I can't believe what they're involved in!" If the truth were told, that statement should be reversed. It should be said, "Parents these days—talk about out of control! I can't believe what they're involved in!" For the most part, we cannot blame our children for our pathetic plight in the realm of household discipline. It rests on the shoulders of moms and dads who have allowed discipline in the home to lapse into a state of anarchy.

The exciting thing, however, is that we can reverse the tenuous tides of that overpermissive ocean. I'm seeing multitudes of moms and dads these days who desire to walk on the solid ground of a disciplined, parent-CEO household. If you are one of those parents, my hope is that this chapter will give you the impetus you need to rein in your out-of-control kids and infuse your home with discipline.

Consider the following statements: "Only fools despise wis-

dom and discipline."[1] "A mother is disgraced by an undisci-
plined child."[2] "Discipline your children, and they will give
you happiness and peace of mind."[3] Did you recognize them?
Those are just a few of the verses from the Bible that emphasize
the importance of discipline in the home. We have already established parenting is the process of teaching and training
your children to leave. And a huge part of that process includes the dilemma of discipline all parents encounter at every
stage of the game.

Any time discipline is discussed, questions arise, debates
break out, and confusion reigns. So I want to set some goals for
this chapter to help you understand where I'm coming from in
this whole area. My first goal is this: I want to help you, not
hammer you. This is a tough subject and a cause of major tension in every home. I want to help alleviate some of that tension rather than add to it.

The second goal is this: I want to come alongside you, not
try to elevate myself above you. I am a fellow struggler. My
wife and I have four children, and 24/7 we are in the midst of
this dilemma called discipline. We are not perfect parents, by
any stretch of the imagination, but we have learned some
things I want to share with you.

The third goal is this: I want to challenge you. I believe
parental potential is unlimited. If we can get a handle on this
subject, the results will be awesome. So, whether you're a pre-
parent, a single parent, a stepparent, or any other kind, I want
to save you boatloads of pain and anxiety by giving you some
help in the area of household discipline.

Especially for Single Parents

Let me push the pause button briefly at this point and address a specific issue single parents face that spills over into the blended family when they remarry. We have so many single parents in society today, and I think you have one of the most difficult and underappreciated roles possible. I have seen so many wonderful things happen over the years, as God has led and touched single parents, giving them power and ability well beyond their years and capacity. I want to share with you, though, several things you need to understand in regard to this single-parent game.

When a divorce occurs, the wife usually experiences a significant cut in personal income. Because the wife is the custodial parent in the vast majority of the cases, her earning potential goes down as she attempts to juggle her work responsibilities with the increased demands of single parenting. The man, on the other hand, experiences a substantial increase in his personal income, because he is then able to devote most of his time to work.

Single moms, throughout this whole scenario, you are especially susceptible to feelings of guilt. You feel guilty for putting your children through the divorce, for being spread too thin between the home and career fronts, and for not being able to do more for your kids financially. Single moms, watch out for this: don't feel so guilty and so bitter that you end up trying to get rid of those feelings by becoming overly permissive with your children. Don't let them do anything because you feel, "Well, if I am extrapermissive, I am making up for these other problems my divorce caused." Your children will suddenly begin to run over you, or you will begin to treat them as if they are peers. Then the authority base is gone.

Let's briefly shift gears to single dads. You feel guilty, single dad, because you aren't as involved with your kids on a day-to-day basis as your ex-wife is. And your guilt leads you to become the purchasing parent. You've got the extra cash, so on weekend visits the entertainment, the excitement, and the adventure are all happening with Dad. You ease the guilt by getting into this sugar-daddy mentality. Again, the authority base disappears, and your kids tumble into a free fall of deteriorating structure and discipline.

A single mom and her three children live a few houses down from ours, and even the casual observer who lives on our street will notice over time a recurring event in that household. Once a week, this woman's ex-husband turns down the street in his black SUV, pulls up to the house, and walks to the door. A few minutes later he comes out with the kids and proceeds to take them to his home for the weekend. One week—this is the quintessential single dad—as he turned the corner, I noticed that in the back of his truck he had brought with him an enormous box from Toys R Us. He drove up to the house as usual, walked to the door, and out came his excited children, saying, "Oh, Daddy's got a new toy. See you, Mom."

Of course, there are also times when this scenario is reversed. Whatever your situation, I urge you to make sure you deal with the guilt between you and God and you and your ex-spouse, so the effects of that guilt don't spill out onto your children. If you are going to mess up, mess up on the side of being too strict, rather than having a permissive mentality that says, "Well, kids, if it feels good, do it. You can do whatever you want and have whatever you want. I just want to make you happy."[4]

Now, let's release that pause button and fast forward to the 411 on discipline.

The Rules of the Game

Friday is my day off. I have a grueling weekend schedule, so I take Fridays to rest and gear up for that. On one particular Friday afternoon several years ago, I was spending some time at home with three of our children—the twins, Laurie and Landra, and EJ. While we were in the garage playing with all the toys, EJ decided he was hungry. I told him he couldn't eat right then because in about an hour we would be having dinner. He said, "Okay, Dad."

He then left the garage and was gone for about five minutes. Upon his return, he was holding a Kudos chocolate-chip granola bar. He asked, "Daddy, can I have this?"

I responded firmly, "EJ, I have just told you that you cannot have anything to eat right now, so put the granola bar back. If you eat it, Daddy will have to discipline you."

He left again, and ten minutes rolled by. I thought, "Surely not!" I started to walk into the kitchen, and while crossing the living room, I discovered the wrapper to a Kudos chocolate-chip granola bar. I got to the kitchen and there was EJ with chocolate drool oozing from the corners of his mouth. When he saw me approaching, he quickly gave an exaggerated swallow, which was so funny to see that I had to bite my tongue to keep from laughing.

I asked, with as much composure as I could muster, "EJ, did you eat that candy bar?" He just looked at me. I repeated, "EJ, did you eat that granola bar?" He wouldn't say anything. I asked once again, "EJ, did you eat this granola bar?" holding up the wrapper in my hand. "Open your mouth. Did you eat this granola bar? Yes or no."

He just repeated what I had said by responding, "Yes or no." Finally he broke, walked over to the steps where he has his time-outs, and sat down. He finally admitted he had eaten the Kudos bar, so he had to suffer the consequences of being disciplined. After I disciplined him—and I must say I was very tempted to back off because he was so cute—we had an excellent time of communication about what he had done wrong and why I had to discipline him.

Discipline—What Is It Good For?

Why did I discipline EJ in this situation? What was the big deal? Would it have been so bad to just let the kid have his granola bar? Well, it all depends on what the goal of discipline is. To help us figure that out, I want to answer two questions in this section: What is discipline? And why do we discipline?

As to the first question, discipline is simply *correction driven by love.* That is the definition of discipline we'll be using in this chapter. We'll see in the coming pages that love and discipline are inseparably linked. Discipline is all about correcting our kids in a way that communicates our great love for them and our desire to see them grow up to be young men and women of great character.

What is the goal of discipline? What does it mean to put the ball through the net? Is the goal of discipline to raise the most intelligent, athletic, or beautiful children? No. The goal of discipline is this: *to mold and shape our children according to their unique, God-given talents and abilities.* In short, it is setting boundaries that produce growth. I believe fighting that battle with EJ on that Friday afternoon produced character growth in his life.

The reason we discipline our children is to help them mature into individuals who reflect the majesty of their Maker. And we have a great role model for the disciplinary process, because God disciplines us. In other words, every time I discipline my children, I'm mimicking my Maker. God is not shy about disciplining us; we should not be shy about disciplining our children. The Bible says clearly, "My child, don't ignore it when the LORD disciplines you, and don't be discouraged when he corrects you. For the LORD corrects those he loves, just as a father corrects a child in whom he delights" (Prov. 3:11–12).

We need to understand something very important: God does not punish his children. Those who have made a commitment to follow Christ and have accepted his gift of forgiveness know Jesus took our punishment on the cross about two thousand years ago. However, as our heavenly Father God does discipline us. God's intention is not to stick it to us when we disobey. He disciplines us out of love for our own protection and we are to discipline our children for the same reason. As James Dobson wrote in his classic book *The New Dare to Discipline,* discipline "is not something parents do *to* a beloved child; it is something done *for* him or her." He went on to add that, whenever disciplining a child, the parent should have this attitude in mind, "I love you too much to let you behave like that."[5]

One of the most loving things we can do for our children is to discipline them. Yet you'll hear a lot of postmodern mumbo jumbo these days, implying that love is positive and discipline is negative. That's laughable at best. There's no way we can love our children compellingly if we are not a source of discipline. And there's no way we can discipline them effectively if we're not a source of love. Love and discipline are tethered together.

Dr. Rosemond related these two qualities this way: "Authority strengthens parental love. Without that strengthening agent, love becomes indulgent and possessive [or overly protective]."[6] When you discipline, Mom, and when you discipline, Dad, you're reflecting the nature and the character of God, who both loves and disciplines us perfectly. If God does it for us—and he's the perfect Parent—then we *must* do it for our children.

Think about the potential here, parents. God has given us our children, and we have the opportunity both to love them and to discipline them. If we do this effectively and strategically, we can literally change the world. And if you don't think the world needs changing, consider the following:

> *Forty-five percent of elementary schools reported one or more incidents of violent crime; the figure balloons to three-quarters of all middle schools (74%). In a typical year, 4% of elementary schools and 19% of middle schools report one or more serious violent crimes (e.g., murder, rape, suicide, use of a weapon, or robbery). . . . One out of every fourteen students is threatened or injured at school with a weapon during a typical school year; one out of every seven students is involved in a serious physical fight on school grounds.[7]*

Parents, out-of-control kids are clearly a serious problem in our world, but discipline, first and foremost, begins at home. If we want to change our schools, our neighborhoods, our streets, and our communities, then we have to change the way we discipline our kids on the family front.

Before we move into some practical ways of doling out discipline in the home, I want first to outline five essential elements that are foundational to parent-CEO discipline. Having a definition for discipline is great. Knowing the goal of discipline is awesome. But we must understand the following elements if we want to put points on the board every day in the disciplinary arena.

The Five Essentials of Discipline

1. Draw Clear Lines

One year, my family and I traveled to the Gulf Coast of Florida with several other families. We had a great time eating out, shopping, and just hanging out at the beach. One couple we were with had a son about the same age as my son. On the beach one afternoon, these two boys challenged their fathers to a game of football. I couldn't help but notice before the game began that these little boys took time to outline the playing field meticulously. They drew end zones in the sand. The sidelines were even lined with decorations. When we played the game, the boys always referred to the boundaries. They told us, "Oh, Dad, you didn't score! See, the line's right there!" or "Oh, you were out-of-bounds over there!" They loved having the lines. The lines made the standards of the game the same for everyone.

None of us would even think about involving ourselves in an athletic contest without boundaries and lines. It wouldn't work. The game would end up in anarchy and chaos. The disciplinary game is no different. We should not even enter the disciplinary arena unless and until we have clearly drawn the lines. When it comes to proper family discipline, we've got to outline the playing field.

The purpose of those lines, however, is not to force our children into acting a certain way. We draw lines so they will learn to make the right choices for themselves as they grow and mature. Remember, discipline is all about producing growth. In their book *Boundaries with Kids,* Drs. Henry Cloud and John Townsend put it this way: "Boundaries with kids isn't about 'making' your child do anything. . . . It is much more about structuring your child's existence so that he experiences the consequences of his behavior, thus leading him to be more responsible and caring."[8]

Once again, when we outline the playing field, we're simply doing what our God has done for us. The Bible is the book that outlines the playing field of life. It shows us how to run, where to run, and what's going to happen to us when we step out of bounds. We've got to do the same thing for our children.

A young mother told Lisa she has listed rules for her children, along with the penalties she will apply when they disobey. She has posted this list on the refrigerator. I think that's genius! Children want lines. They beg for boundaries. Gary Smalley recalled an incident during his own childhood in which his father did not discipline him in the way he expected. He said, "I actually told him that I needed a spanking, but he wouldn't do it. There was something in me that *wanted* to be corrected."[9] We need to set clear lines, then commit to maintaining those boundaries. We also need to understand that children will test our commitment to see if we will move them.

Do you know what an Etch-A-Sketch is? An Etch-A-Sketch is a magnetic art canvas that has two little knobs on the bottom you use to draw shapes, figures, or lines. After you have drawn lines and made shapes, you can shake it, and the objects just disappear. Too many parents are Etch-A-Sketch parents. They will draw lines and then shake the magnetic canvas. They'll draw lines and then shake some more. Then they'll draw some more lines and shake again. The lines, or boundaries, of discipline are always in a state of flux with the Etch-A-Sketch parents. Even though their kids want to know where the lines are, their parents do the Etch-A-Sketch thing. What deserved a penalty last week is okay this week. What was wrong last year is suddenly permissible now. Kids want and need clarity, and we, their parents, are the only ones who can give it to them.

Consider, if you will, the following hypothetical situation. Let's imagine you are watching a professional hockey game. In this game, one of the star players is on a fast break and is flying toward the goal. The crowd is on its feet, cheering and yelling! Everyone can sense that he is going to score. But right before he takes his shot, an opposing player sticks out his skate and trips him, sending him sliding face-first into the wall.

Now, as you would expect, the referee blows his whistle to stop play. At this point, everyone in the arena knows what's going to happen. The referee is going to call a penalty on this guy and send him to the penalty box. But this game is hypothetical. What if, instead of calling a penalty, the referee skates over to the opposing team's player and asks, "Son, did you trip that other player on purpose?" To which the player responds, "No, sir. I didn't do it on purpose." And then what if the referee simply says, "Well, don't do it again. Now, you two hug and play nice, all right?"

Several plays later, one of the other players is pounding an opponent in the head with his stick. This poor guy ends up flat on his back on the ice, nearly unconscious. Now, let's imagine that our referee skates up to this horrible scene occurring right in front of him and says to the player, "Look into my eyes. I'm gonna count! When I get to three, let me tell you something, mister, you're going to be in trouble! I told you we were going out for pizza tonight, but if you don't stop hitting that other player . . . one . . . okay, don't let me get to three! Two!" How ridiculous would it be for those two situations to occur on the hockey rink? The game would be an out-of-control fiasco.

Well, I just described to you the way many parents play the game of discipline. Hockey is a beautiful sport when it's called consistently, but it's an ugly sport if the rules are not clear for everyone. Playing with fuzzy rules can make discipline an ugly game, so we must establish clarity right up front. My point is not that you should not warn your children when they misbehave or that you should never count to three. The issue at hand is whether or not your rules and the consequences for breaking those rules are clearly established. If they aren't, your kids will not take you or your authority seriously.

2. Maintain Consistent Boundaries

Consistency is an essential element of discipline in the home. You need to realize, Mom and Dad, stepparent, or single parent, that our children are begging for consistency. When we're consistent, we're showing our children we are reliable. Our kids realize, "Wow, I can count on Mom and Dad. When I mess up, there's a consequence. From infraction to infraction, from parent to parent, the rules are consistent." Reliability gives our children confidence and strong self-esteem. Those

are things money can't buy. Those are immeasurable invest-
ments no trust fund can touch. And they represent a develop-
mental outcome an Ivy League education can't even touch.

Conversely, if we're inconsistent, like the hypothetical referee I just described, what happens? Children see their parents
as unreliable, and over time the children become insecure and
tentative. In the absence of consistent adult leadership, they
begin to act out and try to control their own world. Everything
in their world suddenly becomes up for grabs.

In contrast to this familial den of disorder, we can teach our
children respect for authority and respect for themselves by
maintaining consistency in our boundaries. In their book
Answering the 8 Cries of the Spirited Child, David and Claudia
Arp said: "Boundaries give children a sense of security—they
let them know what they can and can't do, where they can
and can't go, and how they should or should not behave. . . .
Boundaries also help children learn to be responsible."[10] That's
the agenda, parents—to teach our children responsibility. It's
not to overburden them with silly rules. It's not to give ourselves a head trip by flexing our parental muscles. Good discipline simply gives kids a proper sense of themselves and of the
world around them.

What kind of message are you sending your kids in the way
you discipline them? Are you giving them a sense of security
and confidence in the consistent way in which you enforce the
household rules? Or are you producing feelings of insecurity
through your inconsistency? It's not too late to begin to draw
those lines and maintain them. Certainly, if your kids are
younger, this will be a much easier process. But even if you
have junior-high- or high-school-age kids, you can still develop a household based on both consistent and loving disci-

pline. The longer you wait, though, the harder it will be to initiate and enforce the rule book. Don't put it off until the third or fourth period, after the game has degenerated into a nearly uncontrollable and irreconcilable scene of chaos and confusion.

3. Present a Unified Front

Another essential element of discipline that must be present in the home is that of unity. I think parents know in theory they must present a unified front, but here is how discipline often plays out in reality: in many households, particularly where one parent is a full-time homemaker, that parent is fighting on the front lines, trying to maintain disciplinary order. The kids often view this parent as "the heavy." He or she sees all of the misbehavior during the day, says no about a thousand times, puts the kids in their time-out corner several times, and hears all of the rebellious and sassy smack from the kids. And depending on the level of desperation, he or she may even be running around the house with a wooden spoon in hand.

Conversely, the other parent enjoys more of a cruise director status with the kids. This parent is at work while the other deals with the disciplinary problems of the day. When the parent comes home, he or she is embraced and welcomed and quickly involved in some recreational activity. In fact, you might even hear someone saying, "Welcome aboard the cruise ship *Nondiscipline*. Just kick back and relax, because we're going to have a great time on our cruise this evening."

Or how about this scenario in the two-income family. When the mother comes home from work, the daughter asks her something and the mother says no. Later that evening, the daughter does an end run around Mom and goes to Dad to ask him the same question. (Isn't it amazing how children learn, at a very young age, to play one parent against the other?) In response to his daughter's question, Dad asks, "What did your mother say?" The daughter reluctantly tells Dad that Mom said no.

Dads (or moms, depending on the situation), here is the moment of truth. This is where we cannot and must not cave in. I know it's easy, believe me. You've been at work all day. You're tired and don't want to make this into a big issue. You might even feel a little guilty that you and your spouse are gone so much, so you want to make up for that by giving your kids whatever they ask for. But don't give in, because the kick-backs down the road are brutal.

Whether you are a mom or dad in this scenario, you have to support your spouse and present a unified front. Even if you think, "I disagree with her [him]," you must back your spouse at that moment in front of the kids. Watch her (his) back, be loyal, and show your unity. If you don't agree with the way your spouse is handling discipline, don't say so in front of the kids. Wait until you're alone, then ask, "What were your reasons for making this decision?" or "Why did you feel it necessary to discipline them in this way?" The leaders should not argue with each other in front of the troops. Do it in private. Do it with respect. And do it with the motivation to improve the way you are handling discipline as a team.

Why is it so important to present a unified front? Unity in parental authority and discipline shows your children that you are partners. It shows your children that the marriage relationship—I'll say it again—is the most vital aspect of the home. And we need to model that truth to our kids. You will have your children until they leave home; you will have your spouse for life. Therefore, form an impenetrable front with your permanent partner—your spouse.

4. Consider the Personality Factor

I wrote earlier in the book how strikingly different our four children are, noting especially the amazing difference in personality between our twin daughters, Laurie and Landra. Thinking about that difference takes me back to the Florida vacation I mentioned earlier in this chapter. While on the beach, Landra usually wore what she'd eaten for breakfast and lunch on her swimsuit. She had sand in her hair and coating every inch of her body. When she ran into the ocean to swim, I had to hold her back because she wanted to go deeper and deeper into the water. A friend of mine had a Sea-Doo down there that he let us use, and while riding on it with me several times, Landra said, "Dad, let's go faster! Let's speed! Let's jump the waves!" Landra is my throttle-to-the-firewall daughter.

Her twin, Laurie, is the polar opposite. Laurie spread her towel out neatly on the beach. It would be unthinkable to find Popsicle residue or any other kind of food on her swimsuit. She did not have a grain of sand on her towel, in her hair, or on her perfectly clean body. She even asked her mom to pick her up and carry her from the towel to the ocean so she didn't get sand all over her feet. While swimming, she stayed in the shallow water. And when she rode the Sea-Doo with me (only one time) she had an expression on her face that clearly indicated, "Don't go too fast because you might get me wet!" Laurie is my let's-cruise-in-comfort-and-style daughter.

Given these obvious personality differences, how in the world do I discipline them? That leads us to the fourth essential element of discipline: consider the personality factor. I'm a fellow struggler, and I still haven't cracked this code. But I have learned some important lessons over the years in navigating between these two personalities. For instance, when I discipline Landra, I can't just talk to her in a normal voice. I have to get in her face and speak forcefully and firmly or she'll just zone me out. On the other hand, when I discipline Laurie, all I need to do is talk to her quietly and calmly and she gets it. Sometimes I can just give her a look and she responds.

My father, also Ed Young, has written several books on the topic of parenting. In a chapter on discipline, he described how he had to discipline his three boys in three unique ways. He recalled that with one of his sons, he just had to look at him to get his point across. With another of his sons, all he had to do was talk to him, and he obeyed. But with yet another son, sometimes he had to give him a few swats on the rear end before he got it.[11] Take a wild guess which one I was. That's right—the third one was me.

Let's address for a moment the issue of spanking. Yes, I was spanked on occasion as a child, and I am happy to report, contrary to the recent views of many psychologists and social scientists, I do not harbor any long-standing emotional scars or latent tendencies toward violent behavior. But since corporal punishment—spanking—is such a hotly debated topic, I need to address it at this point in our discussion about discipline.

Time magazine reported in October 2000 on a survey that was conducted with three thousand adults, including 1,066 with children under the age of six. The survey asked these parents whether they thought regular spanking was an acceptable form of punishment. Sixty-one percent said yes.[12]

On the flip side of that survey, the article also cited the

growing disapproval among psychologists, social workers, and pediatricians of spanking as an effective form of discipline. Many of these professionals, the article pointed out, "believe there is a link between spanking and anti-social behavior like cheating and misbehaving. Others worry that childhood spankings enforce children's fear and mistrust of adults, and encourage children to use force themselves." Fortunately, the writer had the insight to differentiate between spanking and child abuse, writing, "A quick swat to the rear-end is hardly analogous to the horrors of beating a child."[13]

What do we make of this? Do we believe the surveys? Do we believe the experts? Do we just follow along with the way our parents disciplined us, many of them using spanking as an acceptable disciplinary alternative? As a pastor, I could easily quote the well-worn adage "Spare the rod, spoil the child" and move on. But I don't believe this issue can be settled that easily. In fact, this saying is attributed to Proverbs 13:24, but no version of the Bible actually translates it exactly that way. Consider the following translation of that verse: "He who spares his rod hates his son, / But he who loves him disciplines him promptly" (NKJV). Or what about the modern New Living Translation: "If you refuse to discipline your children, it proves you don't love them; if you love your children, you will be prompt to discipline them."

Many would argue that the meaning in that verse is *not* literally about using a rod to discipline children, that the word "rod" is a metaphor for, or a representation of, discipline. They would say that employing the "rod of discipline" simply means that to be effective, parents should apply discipline in a consistent and timely manner. The word "rod" is mentioned also in Psalm 23. The psalmist said in verse 4, "Your rod and

Your staff, they comfort me" (NKJV). A "rod" in the Bible is used to guide, to provide, and also to discipline.

Others would say that this verse does indeed suggest that a "rod" or a belt or a paddle is an effective form of discipline. They would agree that parents should administer the discipline in a consistent and timely manner, but they would also say that the "rod" is a *literal* example of an effective form of loving correction. This group would say that, if we do not literally use a rod to discipline our children, we are failing them.

So which way do we go? Which interpretation of this verse is right? You're not going to like my answer to this, but the choice is yours. I believe there is too much ambiguity about this passage for me to say outright, "Yes, we should spank" or "No, we shouldn't." The long and short of it is we each have to make up our own minds based on what we feel is best for our kids. And you know, I think in his infinite wisdom, that's the way God intended it.

We have to evaluate, as parents, whether or not spanking is appropriate for our children given their unique personalities, sensitivities, and wills. That is why I am bringing up this topic of spanking under the personality factor. I believe parents must weigh this issue in light of the tremendous differences in children. The fact is that each child responds differently to different types of discipline, and I cannot tell you whether spanking is or is not appropriate for your child. But if the survey I quoted is accurate, I would hazard a guess that about 61 percent of those reading this book believe that it's okay.

While many child experts disapprove of spanking, many Christian psychologists see it as an acceptable alternative in certain cases, usually as a last resort. I agree with that. Lisa and I spank our children when the offenses they commit call for it. It's not our first option; in fact, it's usually our last. But I think spanking can be an effective form of punishment for children between eighteen months and the teen years. I would personally have a difficult time spanking a child under the age of about eighteen months to two years, depending on the development of the child. Kids that age are not mentally able to understand why they are being spanked, and I believe there are alternative forms of correction that are more effective for that age group.

Spanking is simply one of many options for discipline up to the teenage years. We are going to address many others throughout this chapter. After your kids become teenagers, you have to get really creative! You can add chores or restrict activities—the possibilities are endless. But as we will see later on, the punishment and the crime must meet in order for discipline to be effective. The bottom line is that I do not believe spanking should be our first choice. And it should always be administered lovingly, calmly, and in cases where the child can properly understand why he or she is being spanked.

As to the charge that spanking is child abuse, it is clear that improperly administered spankings can result in abuse. Child abuse happens when parents punish (notice I used the word *punish* rather than *discipline*) their children out of anger. And anger is never, ever appropriate in handing out any form of discipline, spanking or otherwise. We should not speak to our children, spank them, send them to their rooms, give them time-outs, ground them, or anything else out of anger. Instead, we should apply all discipline lovingly and strategically, with the goal of giving correction that results in positive growth. Obviously, there are times when your emotions will get the best of you and we'll address that later on in the section on "Building the Parental Portfolio."

The Strong-Willed Child

One especially difficult personality to deal with is the strong-willed child. If you have been blessed with such a child in your home, you may feel the need to spank her more than you would other children. But just because a child is strong-willed does not necessarily mean you should immediately jump to the last resort of spanking. The strong-willed child often misbehaves just to test your boundaries. Her personality is such that she needs to know where the line of control begins and ends. She will probably not respond very well to subtle hints, voice inflections, that certain look, reasoning, or even yelling. You can try time-outs, grounding, extra chores, and withholding allowance, and she may just grin at you. You may even resort to using the spanking card only to receive a look from her that says, "Is that all you've got?"

Regardless of the method of discipline with strong-willed children, the key is consistency. They must experience a logical consequence for their behavior every time. One article puts it this way: "Strong-willed children learn rules the hard way: by testing them again and again. American psychologist Robert Mackenzie says, 'When our words do not match our actions, children learn to ignore our words and base their beliefs on what they experience.'" All children test rules and boundaries. That's a natural tendency in children. "But," the writer continues, "strong-willed children are more aggressive in their search. 'To them, the word stop is just theory. They want to know what will happen if they don't stop, and they know how to find out,' says Mackenzie. Parents must give them lots of opportunity to experience consistency."[14]

With this particular personality, you must clearly establish the line of authority for the child's own protection. A strong-willed child can become a danger to himself and others through reckless and impulsive behavior if it is not curbed early on. Based on principles from James Dobson's book *The Strong-Willed Child,* one writer gives this advice: "Hold tightly to the reins of authority in the early days, and build an attitude of respect during your brief window of opportunity. You will need every ounce of 'awe' you can get during the years to come. Once you have established your right to lead, begin to let go systematically, year by year."[15]

Our definition of parenting takes on critical importance with the strong-willed child. As you are teaching and training her to leave and become independent, be especially careful to give decision-making rope regularly and strategically or she will rebel, sometimes in dangerous ways. Let her know who is in charge but allow her to make choices whenever possible. Letting her control some things does not mean she is controlling everything or controlling you. Most important, communicate to this child that she is unique and special. She does not want to be ordinary so don't treat her that way. And don't forget to pray, a lot![16]

5. Build the Parental Portfolio

One day, several years ago, I was in a tremendous hurry and running late for a meeting. I was still wearing my running shoes as I raced up to my office, taking the stairs in rapid-fire succession. Well, I should say that I *tried* to take the stairs in rapid-fire succession, because I tripped and whacked my big toe on a concrete step. I'm sure I broke it, because it took weeks to heal. Years later I dropped a barbell on my big toe, breaking it in several places and disfiguring it for good (I'll tell that story later on), so I've not had very good luck in the big toe department.

As with my painful big toe incident, a lot of parents trip up and stub their toes on this last essential element of discipline: the apology. Admit it, Mom and Dad, you have a hard time articulating those two pride-swallowing words to your children when you've made disciplinary mistakes: "I'm sorry." Our children know when we've messed up, fouled up, or fumbled the ball. And in our defense, I believe we are right in the decisions we make for our children about 99 percent of the time. But in that remaining 1 percent, we need to own up to our mess-ups.

When the stock market is going up, people talk about the "bull market." They look at it in amazement and say, "Wow, the stock market is out of sight! That's great. I'm making money. My stocks are going sky high. Just look at my portfolio! Yeah!" Do you realize that children have a mental portfolio when it comes to investing in their parents? Do you want your children to have a bull-market mentality? Do you want their stock in you to go up? Then apologize to them when you are wrong. Your honesty and integrity will pay huge dividends later on in your children's parental portfolios. When you make a mistake, just tell them, "I'm sorry. I want to apologize."

You may have slipped up and done or said something to one of your children out of anger that you regret and feel guilty about. Ask for forgiveness from your child and then make a commitment to cool your jets before taking disciplinary action in the future. They will understand that you're not perfect and will respect you for taking the initiative to mend the relationship.

Maybe you're thinking, "Well, Ed, my children are grown, and the parenting mistakes I made are behind me. It's too late to apologize for those past stumbles." It's not too late. You need to write them a note or call them on the phone. Let them know their forgiveness is important to you. This is so essential, because it communicates to them the value of authenticity and models for them how they should respond to their own kids. God has richly and continuously forgiven you and me. We should take the value of that reconciliation and seek forgiveness with our children.

The Significant Seven

Lisa and I have been married for more than twenty years and we have four beautiful children. Over the years I've had the privilege of speaking to literally thousands of teenagers, children, and parents on the subject of discipline. And through those experiences as a parent, pastor, and communicator I've come up with what I call the Significant Seven. These are seven aspects of discipline from the Bible that will show us how to discipline on the rugged plains of parental reality. These aspects flow from the five essential elements we just discussed and take us farther into the day-to-day practice of disciplining our kids. I truly believe if we apply them appropriately, they can do some great things. They have been a godsend for my family and I want to share them with you with the confidence that they can be a help in your home as well.

1. Start Soon So You Won't Raise a Loon

I drove by a restaurant not too long ago by the name of Loons on a Limb. As I passed it, I thought, "That's what a lot of parents are raising these days: loons on a limb." Do you know why so many parents are raising loons? They aren't following the biblical definition of parenting we have been developing throughout this book. Deuteronomy 6 and Proverbs 22 give us clear instruction that we are to prepare our children from the very beginning of their lives to leave the home. From infancy on, we are preparing them little by little—emotionally, physically, mentally, and spiritually—to go out someday and begin lives of their own.

Too many ill-informed parents are raising loons because they aren't modeling God's truth on a daily basis. They are not training their kids in the way they should go when they leave the comfort and security of Mommy and Daddy's home. And much of that preparation centers on the theme of this chapter: discipline. We need to give our children discipline early and often if they are going to fire on all cylinders as single adults, as married adults, and as parents in the future.

If we don't get serious about this now, our children will be out in the world someday, floating on the seas of relativism, just hanging like loons on limbs, wondering what life's all about. They'll be totally insecure. They'll see us as unreliable. And they'll lack the confidence to be and do all that God wants for them, because we did not capture the moment and begin to discipline them early in their lives.

So, in this first installment of the Significant Seven aspects of discipline, let me give you some profound advice: Start now. Start now! Start now! Start now! Is that clear enough? I don't care if your child is in the cradle or in the driver's seat of a Mustang, you must begin to instill in him or her the benefits of a disciplined life. Of course, it's a given that the earlier you start, the better, but it is never too late to make a positive change. I implore you, before we go any farther, to make a game plan, draw the lines, and commit to maintaining those boundaries with your kids.

I know it's not going to be easy to make these changes in your home, but "It's too hard" is no excuse. When your children are loons hanging on limbs someday, I don't think you want to have to explain to them, "I'm sorry we didn't discipline you more, but it was just too much work." That's not going to cut it then, and it doesn't cut it now. Parenting is not easy. Discipline is hard. But I promise you, the earlier you start, the easier it will be later on.

2. Discipline for Motivation, Not Humiliation

Just like the entire process of parenting, discipline should take advantage of the teachable-moment methodology. Specifically, some of the greatest teachable moments and the best opportunities for communication occur during and after a disciplinary event. The purpose of these times is to teach children and motivate them, not to humiliate them. With that in mind, an important motivational principle to remember is to discipline in private, not in public. Public discipline is humiliating, degrading, and counterproductive to real growth.

You may argue, "Ed, what if my kid's going nuts in a restaurant? I don't have any other choice but to get in his face in front of the staff and the patrons." My response is you do have another choice. Take the child to the rest room or outside the restaurant and talk to him or her privately. Say something like this before you apply discipline: "I love you too much, and God loves you too much, to allow you to get away with this behavior." Then explain what the consequences are for acting up, whether it's a time-out, a grounding, no dessert, an early bedtime, a spanking (if warranted), or whatever you decide. This is much more effective, I believe, as a teaching tool when it is done in private and not in public, during the heat of the moment. You are likely to cause an even bigger scene by saying or doing things you regret later.

3. When You Give In, No One Will Win

While eating out with my wife one evening, I saw a man with his family at the table next to us. A few minutes into the meal, the little boy at the table began acting up—throwing a temper tantrum and talking back to his mother. While all of this was happening, I had my eye on the father to see what he would do. That muscular man, who looked as if he could start for most NFL teams, gave in to the demands of a little boy about a quarter of his size. This poor, whipped father pathetically cowered to his sassy son.

As I thought about what was really happening in that situation, I realized that he was simply trying to avoid a difficult conflict by taking the easy way out. Sound familiar? What happened to that father is a major temptation for all parents. They think, "It's much easier just to give in than to try to win." But the truth is this: when you give in, *no one* will win.

Here's what this father didn't understand, and what many other parents today don't understand as well: when you avoid conflict with your child, you're actually signing up for more and more conflict later on. It's better to deal with an issue when it comes up rather than waste time by having to revisit the incident farther down the road. That principle is true in all areas of leadership, not just parenting. If, as a leader, you do not definitively deal with an issue when it first surfaces, it will keep resurfacing until you do deal with it. And each time it comes up, it will be harder to handle.

Young children especially need to have disciplinary problems dealt with as immediately as possible. You cannot come back to them three days after an incident and decide that it's finally time to deal with it. Now, if you are angry or overly emotional you may need to wait an hour or two to make sure that a cooler head prevails. But as a rule, kids need and want immediate resolution when they disobey.

I am not trying to be demeaning or flippant with this next illustration, but please hang with me while I explain. One Monday morning at 7:30 A.M. I walked out the front door of my home to go to work. Every time I leave for work in the morning, I intuitively note that I need to negotiate something I call the Drool Zone. I have two massive bullmastiffs with a combined weight of about three hundred pounds who take slobbering to another level. One brush against my pant-leg or clothing and I have to go back inside and change clothes.

As I approached my truck on that particular morning, I saw something unfolding before my eyes that shocked me. My two dogs, Brute and Apollo, had their mouths wrapped around the four feet of chrome that ran along the driver's side of the truck I owned at the time, and they were pulling it off with their teeth. Needless to say, Daddy was not happy. I scolded them.

In fact, I tried to chase them down so I could restrain them in the backyard, but they eluded my grasp. So I had to settle for yelling a few well-chosen words of discipline in their general direction: "What are you doing? No! Bad doggies! I don't like that."

I got in the truck, and as I made my commute to the office, other people on the freeway were pointing at the side of my truck to make sure I knew a four-foot piece of chrome was hanging loose. These people obviously didn't realize I owned a couple of truck-eating dogs. The story, though, believe it or not, continues. The next day at about 9:30 P.M., Lisa and I and the kids drove up our driveway in the truck. I parked where I always do, in front of the garage. (We had so many toys in the garage that I didn't even try parking there.) As we got out of the truck, Lisa asked in a sweet voice, "What would you think about pulling the truck inside the garage so the dogs won't tear it up again?"

I said, "Lisa, I watch Animal Planet, and I scolded the dogs. I told them no and that I didn't like what they did. They will not touch my truck. Trust me."

You guessed it. One hour later, the chrome on the other side of the truck had been ripped off. I actually have a picture, documented evidence of Apollo and Brute with the chrome in their mouths. Obviously we had a disciplinary problem. There was a breakdown of some sort in the disciplinary process. I did not effectively correct their behavior, and as a result they went right back and did it again.

Parents, the amount of money spent and time lost due to ineffective discipline and miscommunication is staggering. Just as I failed to deal effectively and immediately with my dogs' misbehavior, we do the same thing over and over again

with our children. I'm not trying to compare kids with ca-
nines, but I think you get my point. If you give in too easily or
avoid handling the conflict when it occurs, no one wins. And
you cannot let that happen. Don't assume you have dealt with
the problem; know for sure that you have by doing what needs
to be done when it needs to be done.

4. Get Proper Pay When They Disobey

The fourth of the Significant Seven aspects of discipline is to
get proper pay when your kids disobey. You do this by making
sure the sentence you dole out matches the crime your kids
committed. In other words, the disciplinary action must fit the
infraction. Here are a couple of things we've done in our
home.

One time one of our children was having a struggle with
selfishness. She didn't understand two things: one, everything
she has comes from God, and two, everything God graciously
gives her comes through the hands of her parents. Lisa and I
talked about it, and we decided that she needed to learn that
Mom and Dad "giveth" and Mom and Dad "taketh away." So
the best form of discipline, given that particular child committing that particular infraction, was to take away her favorite
outfit for ten days. She got the point and began to loosen her
grasp and share her things with others.

Another time, I was lying on my bed doing some studying
in the master bedroom. One of my children—I will not name
which one—without knowing I was in my bedroom, walked
into the bathroom and said a bad word. I stood up and walked
into the bathroom, to my child's shock, and asked, "What did
you say?" Then, as the discipline for cursing, I took some soft
soap and washed out the child's mouth. I can assure you, that

child thought long and hard before using a curse word again. We can be creative when we discipline, can't we?

Are your kids giving proper pay when they disobey? If they throw food at the dinner table, maybe they should miss dessert. If they talk smack to you, maybe they need to write an essay on the meaning of the Fifth Commandment, "Honor your father and mother." If they break something you told them not to touch, maybe they need to go without their allowances until they've paid for it. If they sneak out and go to a party you said they couldn't attend, maybe they need to be grounded for two weeks without TV privileges. Parents, you be the judge, but discipline that is effective is creative and matches the infraction.

5. Call It Tight, and You'll Do Them Right

If you're going to err, err on the side of strictness, not leniency. I'm not implying that we need to be militaristic-type parents. I already gave you my opinion on that when I described the NCAA parents in the second chapter. But my experience as a parent has taught me that it's much easier to loosen the reins after being strict than it is to tighten the reins after the horse has already gone wild.

I've seen the reality of that same principle in many other areas of life and leadership. Take the workplace, for instance. I am the senior pastor of a large church with about nineteen thousand people attending on the weekends and a staff of over 150. I have found, time and time again, that when we make policies that are too loose, too informal, or too lenient, it is very difficult to move to a stricter rule. Whether we are dealing with vacation benefits, work hours, dress code, Christmas bonuses, sick leave, insurance benefits, or you name it, people almost always react negatively when you tighten up the ship, because they feel you are taking away certain rights to which they are entitled.

On the other hand, when you begin with a firmer hand, you can provide more and more leniency as you feel the people in your charge can handle it. As you do, they will appreciate the added benefits and privileges you are giving them, because they view your loosening of the reins as a reward for responsible behavior, not as a right.

Kids react the same way. They should feel your loosening of restrictions is a reward for their growing maturity and responsibility, rather than expecting it as something you owe them. As they begin to prove to you that they can handle additional freedom, you can give it to them. But if you begin with a free-for-all home environment, you have nowhere to go but toward more restrictions. Teachers employ this same principle in the classroom. During the first few weeks of school, they are very strict. Then as the students respond appropriately, they can lighten up the rules. It is always, always harder to go stricter than it is to go softer.

A major key to this mind-set is remembering most of what we give our kids are privileges they need to earn, not rights they can expect. This realization prepares our children for the truth that nothing worthwhile in life comes easily.

If you call it tight, they'll end up right. One of the incredible benefits of starting out tight is that your kids will appreciate the freedom you give them. They will savor so much more all the things they have been given in life. Think of the power of gratitude. What would it feel like to have your kids show you appreciation for all the money you've spent on them—for the clothes on their backs, the food on the table, and the roof over their heads? How great would it be if they were thankful for the little privileges and perks they enjoy every day under your guidance and protection: to be able to go out and play, to watch TV, to go on vacations, to go out to eat, to play sports, to take piano lessons, to take ballet lessons, to attend church activities and learn about God, to have a bowl of ice cream, to enjoy the company of a pet, to be surrounded by toys and video games and bikes and trains?

Are you encouraging this attitude of gratitude in your children by showing appreciation to God? Do you thank him together as a family for the little privileges he gives you every day? Or are you teaching your kids to complain, "Oh, it's not fair. I wish I had this or I wish I had that. *They* have it! I should get it, too!" One of the greatest signs of spiritual maturity is an attitude of gratitude. And one of the best ways to teach our children to appreciate what they have in life is to model thankfulness to God for his mercy and grace in our own lives.

Think of how God has dealt with humankind throughout history. He began his relationship with the Israelites in the Old Testament with very strict, regimented laws. He required absolute obedience to this moral code. But then think of the sacrifice God made through Jesus Christ and the incredible freedom that provides for us. Christ did what we could not do—he fulfilled his Father's requirements with absolute perfection. Think of how he has given us so much more than we deserve. We deserve punishment, but he gives us forgiveness. Do you appreciate that? The incredibly tight restrictions of God's law should give a much greater appreciation for his equally incredible grace. Do you have a real appreciation for the freedoms and privileges you have as his child?

Teach your children to appreciate God, and teach them to appreciate you. The results will be unbelievable.

6. When You're Specific, They'll Be Terrific

One night Lisa and I hired a sitter for the kids so we could go out on a date. I was still fairly green at the parenting thing at the time and had not learned the value of specific instructions. So this is what I told our children before we left: "Okay, kids, make sure to behave. Bye."

What was that? Behave? I should have said, "You do what the sitter tells you to do. After you eat the pizza, help her clean up. And then go to bed when she tells you to go to bed." Fortunately for our baby-sitters, I've learned since then to be more specific when we leave our children.

Gary Smalley has suggested that one of the most important factors in raising children is "establishing clearly defined and understood rules in the home, limits that children know they cannot violate without some consequence."[17] So many children are running around these days without knowing the details of what Mom and Dad expect of them. They don't know the specific boundaries or have the clarity needed to achieve success. So my question as a parent is: how can we discipline our kids if we have not told them specifically what we want them to do? Do your kids a favor. Give them clear, detailed instructions, then let them achieve small successes throughout the day as they fulfill your expectations. Your kids will feel better about themselves, and you will not feel the need to discipline them as often.

7. A Bribe Sends a Bad Vibe

Consider this little scenario actress Sharon Stone recounted on *The Late Show with David Letterman* on September 10, 2003.

Sharon told a story about taking her three-year-old son on an overnight camping trip. They got to the campsite, set up the tents, and later in the evening settled down for the night. But there was a small problem: her son was afraid of the dark.

She tried to console him by telling him they could sleep with the light on. But that didn't work. "It is still dark outside," he informed her, and he wanted to go home. Consoling didn't work, so she moved on to reason. Sharon took her son outside and showed him the darkness, telling him, "It's dark out here, but it's light inside where we are, so there's nothing to be afraid of." But reasoning didn't work; he still cried and wanted to go home. Next came bribery. First she tried candy, but candy did not appease him. The last resort was to bribe him with money. Yes, she tried to bribe her three-year-old with money, and shock of all shocks, money held no interest for the distraught toddler. He continued to cry and whine and complain. Finally—you guessed it—she gave in to him, packed up the campsite, and went home.

Does that sound familiar? We can't be too hard on Sharon Stone, because we've all experienced something very similar. Most likely, you've played the same kind of tug-of-war with your kids numerous times. I've tried to bribe my kids, and it has never worked to the extent that I had hoped. In fact, I have found that a bribe feeds the kid-CEO household in a big way. When you bribe, you have turned control over to the kids. They then have the leverage; you don't. Instead of doing what you say just because you are the parent and they are supposed to obey you, they do what you say only when there is something in it for them.

We saw in the first chapter why children should obey their parents. Remember Ephesians 6:1: "Children, obey your parents because you belong to the Lord, for this is the right thing to do." It doesn't say, "Children, obey your parents only if the pot is sweet enough, if it's really worth your while." A bunch of lawyers didn't draft this principle. Don't look for any escape clauses or fine print in the Bible. It is simple and direct: obey.

Ephesians goes on to say this: "This is the first of the Ten Commandments that ends with a promise. And this is the promise: If you honor your father and mother, 'you will live a long life, full of blessing'" (6:2–3). Isn't that great? Our loving God gives us a promise, then the perks of the promise. The writer was referring here to wellness and longevity. These days people are always talking about being well and living longer. If we want our kids to be well and to live long, it all goes back to obeying us and honoring us as father and mother.

When a child honors his or her father and mother, he values *and* respects them, with both his attitudes and actions. Many children have little comprehension of this notion. Parents, on the other hand, oftentimes have difficulty understanding how to teach this concept. It's good for children to say that they love their parents. I'm all for that. Good for them. But how do we, as parents, teach our children to *show* it? The answer is with our own attitudes and our own actions. We must model for our children the loving attitudes, the facial expressions, the character, the persistence that we want to see in them. In turn, they will reciprocate those things to us.

Children need us, as parents, to take charge. It is our responsibility to teach our children discipline, and God has given us several tools to do just that. Here's the real key, though, to effective discipline—I've saved this for last because it's the most important factor: if we want to hit it out of the park in the area of discipline, we must as parents be people of discipline. If we want to instill the benefits of a disciplined life in our children, we must submit to the discipline of our heavenly Father. When we humble ourselves before God and receive his correction, we will be leaps and bounds ahead of the game in giving correction to our kids. It all goes back to the family flow chart. Get in line under God, and your kids will get in line under you.

PART FIVE

Structure

Raising
Well-Rounded
Kids

{ 8 }

The Parent Zap

MEET THE BUSYLEYS. The Busyleys are a family on the go. It's difficult even to have a long or meaningful conversation with them because they move too fast. The most you hear from them is, "Hi! Bye! Gotta get going—see ya later!" They are constantly traveling to this event or carpooling to that program. The Busyleys are sleep deprived, overscheduled, and exhausted. They don't spend much time relaxing in their house; they treat it more like a pit stop than the center of family life.

Technology supports the NASCAR-type pace the Busyleys maintain—they rely on anything they think will make a certain task easier or faster. The faster everything can be done, the better it is for the family. That way, they might be able to cram yet another activity into their already overbooked schedule.

As a result of this heavy schedule, the Busyleys go through life with the belief that everything should revolve around the children. The children are not only the central focus in the family, they are the *only* focus. Mom and Dad sacrifice whatever they need to just to satisfy their kids. If the children have an activity at the same time that the parents do, then Mom and Dad sacrifice their social life. When it comes to a choice between spending time together as a couple on a Friday night or taking the kids to the mall, it's "Pack up the minivan! The kids want to go to the mall again." Their relational life runs a distant second to their kids' wants, needs, and desires.

And what about intimacy? Well, they simply chalk that up as another sacrifice on the alter of children's activities. To these parents, intimacy and parenting don't fit in the same sentence, let alone the same house. In essence, *everything* the children want to do is a priority, and the parents will pull out all the stops to keep them happy.

The Race Is On

The Busyleys represent an alarming trend on the family front over the last several decades. The home has essentially lost its place as the hub of family activity. Instead, the family has become mobile, and the product of that mobility is that millions of moms and dads are feeling overwhelmed by all of their children's activities. The family schedule has boiled over beyond reasonable expectations. Parents feel incarcerated in their minivans or SUVs—literally belted down as they chauffeur their kids from activity to activity. They cart their kids around to school, music lessons, soccer practice, dance lessons, Boy Scouts, Brownies, and baseball games. And if there's any time left over after all of that, they *may* squeeze in church on the weekend. In effect, what used to be affectionately referred to as the Parent Trap has morphed into the Parent Zap.

Why are so many families these days running at this pace?

Why are they so zapped? Why are they enslaved to their frantic and frenetic schedules? A *Newsweek* magazine article compared raising children in today's world to competing in a triathlon with no finish line in sight. And from my vantage point, that seems to be a pretty good analogy. In the article, Stephanie Coontz, professor of history and family studies at Evergreen State College in Olympia, Washington, said that a lot of people are parent zapped because of the technological and digital revolution our society is undergoing. She believes that parents today are reacting to the technological changes the same way parents during the Industrial Revolution did.

During the 1820s the blacksmiths, farmers, and other laborers were scared their children would not be able to withstand the transition of the day. Their fear was in how their children would handle all of the anticipated free time and new opportunities the introduction of machinery into society would provide. Parents back then wanted their children to take advantage of every possible opportunity but often didn't know how to provide guidance and balance in a changing and confusing world.

Ms. Coontz wrote, "Parents today are having a comparable anxiety crisis." Parents today are making the same decisions parents then made. She says we are trying to overcompensate for the time that technology saves. Parents fear their children will miss out on opportunities, so they "sacrifice their [own] dwindling free time to make sure their kids are safe and want for nothing."[1] In other words, technology has provided more free time and opportunities for our kids but parents aren't sure what to do with them. As a result, oftentimes an endless line of activities fills the schedule, squeezing out meaningful time for both marriage and family.

Unsure of how to provide balance in a confusing technological age of endless options, we think we must have every little blank space on our calendars filled. It doesn't start with our signing up for ten or fifteen different things, though. It starts off in a very benign fashion, with just a couple of activities penciled in on the schedule. Then, if we don't keep our calendars in check, if we don't monitor our time, it can get eaten up. Before we realize it, we can have so many activities and programs on our agenda that we allow the big hairy calendar monster to swallow all of our time and energy. When we don't allow for any downtime in our lives, and we go through life as if we're in a NASCAR race, we end up forgetting about the most important things in life. Without taking proactive steps to spend our time wisely, it is easy to let our schedule get skewed and our lives messed up.

The Gift of Time

In my book *High Definition Living,* I described things that steal our time as "minute muggers."

> *Minute muggers are those insignificant things that steal the minutes from our day. Sometimes we foist them on ourselves, and sometimes they're delivered by other people. They seem to attack me every day. I'm just working along trying to be organized, and* bop! *I get mugged. And then, at the end of the day, I find myself asking, "Where did the time go?"*[2]

Time is a gift from God. As with all of God's gifts, we are to be good stewards of what he has given us.

The fact is, though, we have all misspent our gift in one way or another. In today's culture, as much as ever before, frenzied families are guilty of this. Activities that we involve ourselves in seem to multiply like rabbits. We occupy our time and that of our children with so many commitments that a lot of parents end up making two major mistakes.

The first mistake we make is *we forget that activities are supposed to be fun for our kids.* The primary purpose of getting our children involved in different sports and lessons is to let them learn and enjoy whatever that activity may be. But we make the mistake of taking the fun out of it by overscheduling and by taking everything they do so seriously. Many times, these activities become something they *have* to do rather than something that they look forward to doing.

The second mistake we make regarding activities is *we begin to micromanage our kids' lives.* Rather than allowing them to enjoy an activity, we begin to control them according to our own agenda and where it could take them in life. Our eyes glaze over with visions of potential success. In effect, we become their agents instead of their parents.

Steinbergitus

Leigh Steinberg, one of the world's most successful sports agents to date, has managed the lives of many of the greatest athletes in professional sports. The basic responsibility of a sports agent is to represent an athlete when it comes time to draft a contract. The agent is the person in the meetings who pushes for more money, better benefits, and guarantee clauses in case of any unforeseen accidents. He or she manages nearly every aspect of the athlete's professional life.

A lot of parents have Steinbergitus, and they don't even realize it. These parents manage their children's lives the way a sports agent manages his clients. They push their children, thinking the push will drive them to the next level. These parents think, "One day my kid will make it to the big stage, the silver screen, the professional athletic field, or the executive boardroom. I will see to it that she gets there. After all, it's *my* vision, and I'm going to make it happen." They ultimately turn the entire focus away from the original intention of enjoyment, thinking that if they push hard enough, then their children will "make it."

And the media only helps to feed this disease. We continually hear stories about how the parents of stars pushed these superstars when they were children and how much they sacrificed within the family. Stories like these give us the idea that stardom is made, not given by the grace of God. They tell us that, in order to be highly successful, you have to start early, be intentional, push hard, and sacrifice everything. We're told that if we follow that formula, we can make a superstar out of our child.

The Projection Symptom

A few symptoms will help to determine if you are carrying this disease. The first is one I call the Projection Symptom. Oftentimes parents who have Steinbergitus project their own junk from the past onto the shoulders and lives of their children. These parents try to live out their unfulfilled dreams through their kids. Whatever it is they failed to accomplish in life, they push their kids to accomplish. And although it may be apparent to others, these parents often don't realize they are doing it.

The Projection Symptom effectively circumvents the entire goal of parenting. The final chapter of this book will address what we are trying to do as parents in helping our kids develop their unique and God-given abilities and talents. But let me just emphasize one thing here: if you are trying to live some unrealized fantasies through your kids, you are not fulfilling your fundamental role as a parent. Your job is to guide your children in the way God has uniquely gifted them, not in the way *you* want them to be. Remember, your child is an individual, not a client. Let her discover her own dreams and visions for her life, and then help her accomplish them in God's good time.

The Pro Symptom

Another symptom of Steinbergitus is the Pro Symptom. Moms and dads with this symptom believe, deep down in their hearts, that if they push hard enough, their children will make it to the professional arena. This can be especially true when it comes to sports, modeling, or music. They rationalize their zeal with examples of current stars. They say things like, "I've seen *Behind the Music*. I saw what those parents did with their daughter when she was small, so I'm going to do the same thing for my daughter. That way, she can become a superstar." Or "My son is pretty good at golf. And if I just do what that golfer's dad did, then he can make it into the PGA. I think I could push him to do it."

When I was younger, I was a pretty good basketball player. In fact, I was good enough to start on the junior varsity team of the largest high school in South Carolina when I was in only the eighth grade. And when I was in the tenth grade, I started on the varsity team as point guard. Universities from around the country offered me scholarships to come play for them after I graduated. I averaged around twenty points per game in high school, and I thought, "Ed, you're good! You might make it to the NBA someday."

One year during high school, I attended an invitation-only basketball camp. Only the top 180 players east of the Mississippi River were invited to go, so I thought I was something special. Before I went, I thought I would go into the camp and annihilate any competition from the other guys. But reality hit when I was standing in the registration line. I looked around at the size and strength of the other kids, and I knew that I wasn't going to annihilate anything. I said to myself, "Ed, you have picked the wrong sport, brother! You are out of your league!" Some of those guys were six-foot-five or taller—in high school! Before we even held a single practice at the camp, I knew that my dreams of making it in the NBA were dashed.

Then, during the camp, that certainty was reaffirmed. With all of these high-school all-American players there, Hubie Brown, a legendary NBA coach, stood up and said, "You know what? There might be one, maybe two, of you who will make it in the NBA." The rest of us were just left dreaming.

Parents, I think it's great for you and your children to have dreams of stardom, whether it's in sports, music, drama, or some other venue. But the chances of their achieving celebrity status are fairly poor, no matter how talented they are. If they do go on in life to hit the big time, that's fantastic. But it's not up to us whether our children are highly successful. It is in God's hands. He is the one who decides who does and does not "make it." So don't try to wrest that responsibility away from God's hands.

I am not indicating we should not introduce our children to a variety of activities. I'm not even implying we should not encourage our children to pursue something they're interested in and give it everything they've got. I think it's a positive influence to expose them to a wide range of activities. And by all means, if they are good at something, cheer them on. Who knows, you *may* just have the next Celine Dion or Michael Jordan or Tiger Woods. But please be prepared for the reality that you probably don't. And most important, love your kids for who they are and the special roles God has for them and only them.

The Pride Symptom

Another sign that you might have Steinbergitus is the Pride Symptom. In order to recognize whether we have this, parents, we need to take a long, hard look in the mirror. We have to ask ourselves, "Why have I made such an insane schedule for my kids? Why am I freaking out over their involvement in all these programs and activities? Am I really pushing for the good of my children or am I doing it for myself?"

So often, the truth is that we are doing it all for ourselves. We want to be able to say to our friends, "My kid is involved in this and that. My kid is the fastest. My kid is the smartest. My kid is . . ." We crave the little ego boosts we get by giving the impression our child is somehow better than our friends'. And the power of pride pushes us to drive our child even more.

Pride is the first of what we have come to know as the Seven Deadly Sins. I wrote a book several years ago entitled *Fatal Distractions,* in which I described each of these sins. In the book I called them "obstacles that mess up our lives" and gave practical advice for overcoming them. But pride has a unique place on this list, because it is the precursor of all the other deadly sins. Pride is the breeding ground for anger, envy, slothfulness, lust, gluttony, and greed. It was pride that tripped up the great angel Lucifer (Satan) and caused him to be thrown out of heaven, along with a third of the angels, who had followed his misguided rebellion. In the beginning of creation, it was pride that tempted Adam and Eve to disobey God and eat of the forbidden fruit, bringing the curse of sin to all humanity. The temptation that was presented to them was to eat the fruit and be like God. They weren't content to be created in the image of God, because pride always wants more. They thought they knew better than God. The proud person says, "I know what's best for me." They didn't want God ruling in their lives; they wanted to *be* God. And that was and is the ultimate mark of pride.

And parents, it is pride that has the potential to bring you, your kids, and your entire family down. It's okay to be proud of your kids and their accomplishments. You should give your kids a regular pat on the back and words of encouragement. But if you let them, the excesses of pride have the potential to make you lose perspective. You replace God's priorities for your family with the gods of winning, success, and achievement. Pride is a dangerous thing and a particularly ugly symptom of Steinbergitus.

Mom and Dad, if you can honestly look at yourselves in the mirror and identify these symptoms, you probably have Steinbergitus. But identifying the disease is only half the battle. Not only do we need to be able to recognize if we are carriers of the disease, we also need to find out how to get rid of it and arm ourselves with a strong prevention method to keep it at bay.

The best family experts around have written hundreds of

books on the frazzled family. Libraries are packed with this information. There are several places we can go and differing viewpoints on what we can do to morph our frenzied family into a focused family. But God's organizational design for the family has already laid the groundwork we need concerning our time management, our priorities, and our focus in life. What we need to do is to take some of this sound, biblically based advice and apply it to our lives. When we follow these suggestions, they will bring sanity back into our schedules. We can capture this gift called time in the most strategic way possible.

Don't OD on Options

The first piece of advice we need to follow is *Don't OD on options*. In today's world, we have many, many options available to us. When we walk into Starbucks, we have the choice of sizes for our coffee—tall, vente, or grande. Then we can choose whether we want a double or triple shot of espresso to go with it, light foam or no foam, soy milk or whole milk, cinnamon or cocoa sprinkles—the list seems to be limitless. Just the other day I saw a huge sign hanging outside of a local convenience store that read "1,300+ ways to create your coffee." (I thought the plus sign was especially amusing, as if 1,300 ways weren't enough.)

All of these options are great, but we don't opt for everything at Starbucks. The same should be true in our families' lives. Too many of us think, "If I don't have my child in every single activity she can possibly be involved in, she might miss an opportunity." Well, you *are* going to miss something if you overschedule your family. But it will be much more devastating than missing a season of soccer or a Girl Scout campout. If you try to choose everything, you will miss out on the best thing.

In the Book of Luke, one of Jesus' friends, a woman named Martha, was freaking out about having Jesus over for dinner. She was preoccupied with getting everything just right. In other words, she was OD-ing on options. While Martha ran around the house, worrying herself about preparing a lavish meal for Jesus, her sister, Mary, was sitting at Jesus' feet and listening to him teach. Martha was upset that Mary wasn't helping her, and at first glance, you might think she had a point. But rather than getting on Mary's case for her apparent laziness, look at what Jesus said: "Martha . . . you are worried and upset about many things, but only one thing is needed. Mary has chosen what is better, and it will not be taken away from her" (10:41–42 NIV). The best thing for Mary and Martha was to sit at the feet of Jesus and learn from him while he was still with them, rather than frantically trying to fix a big meal.

Are you choosing the best for your family, or are you, like Martha, OD-ing on options? It's time to get serious about selecting the best things and letting all the others go. When you fail to be deliberate about the options you choose, you allow calendar confusion to set in and reign over your home.

The God Grid

"If you don't state your priorities, then someone else will." That's a saying that you may already be familiar with, but I would like to add an addendum to that philosophy. Someone other than ourselves has already set our priorities. His name is

God. And we have already seen what his priorities are for the family: God, marriage, and then kids.

So our job, parents, is not to set the priorities for our family. Our job is to set parameters, guidelines, and guardrails for our children based on the priorities that God has already laid out for us. We do that so that our children can become the kind of people he wants them to become by utilizing their own skill sets.

We have a critical role in the development of our children. We are here to help guide them. It's not a popularity contest, parents. It is, though, an opportunity to raise our children the way God desires, and many are doing an unbelievable job at this. But it all comes back to the priorities and options that we choose to pursue in our lives and the lives of our children.

When you are faced with all these options and choices in life, what should you do? The best way to decide whether or not to pursue an opportunity is to run it through what I call the God Grid. When a prospect presents itself to you, ask yourself some questions: "How will this activity affect my relationship with God and my involvement with the local church? How will it affect the intimacy, the connection I have with my spouse? How will it affect my relationship with my kids? Will they be able to handle the stress this activity may cause?" Until we begin to sift seriously through our options, we will never understand what priorities are all about or how we should spend our time on this earth.

The first year in many years that the Dallas Mavericks basketball team made the playoffs, a friend invited me to go to one of their postseason games. The game was scheduled on a Saturday afternoon at 2:00. I speak twice every Saturday evening at our 5:00 and 6:30 services, but I thought there would surely be enough time to get back from the game. I am an avid basketball fan, so my initial response when he invited me was "Yes!" I jumped at the chance.

Then I began to think about the decision I had made. I ran it through the God Grid. I looked at the priorities God had placed in my life—himself, spouse, children. I remembered how intense the weekends were, even without having additional activities scheduled. I knew I needed to work for at least six hours before I spoke that Saturday evening. And I thought about the next Sunday morning and the three services I had to prepare for that day. I remembered that our children had basketball in the afternoon, which I coached for two hours. I also remembered that every other Sunday evening, my wife and I met with our Bible study group, which took another three hours of the weekend.

After running all the options through the God Grid, I thought, "Going to the Mavericks game is a good option. But against the backdrop of all that is going on during the weekend, it is not the best option." So I called my friend and told him, "Thank you for the invitation, but I have to say no. Maybe I will be able to do it another time." I had to decline this good thing because God had placed bigger priorities in my life.

That is how God helps me decide what options in life to choose and which ones to let go. I have to look in the mirror daily and ask him, "How does this option square up with your priorities for my life?" There is no use discussing what our priorities should be. We should not be praying for God to tell us what our priorities are. They are already mapped out for us. Our prayer should be, "God, help me to *apply* your priorities to my life so I will be able to choose the right options every day."

As we think about how to use the God Grid to choose only the best from all of the good things out there, let me make a few suggestions to help you navigate through the many options available to you and your family.

Use a Kid Lid

One of our favorite things to do as a family is to go out to eat. When we visit a restaurant with all of our kids, it is more like an invasion than a dining experience. It's not uncommon for the people sitting around our table to bolt when they see us coming, especially if they are trying to have a romantic dinner. For some reason, they are not excited about seeing a family of six sit down next to them. People have this idea that kids are going to make a lot of noise, disrupt their conversation, and maybe even spill their food or drinks all over the place. That's why, over the years, we have learned that when we order something to drink for our younger children, we don't allow them to have regular glasses. That would be asking for trouble. Instead, we ask our server to put the "kid lid" on the glass. With a kid lid covering the glass, the cup could fall to the ground and not spill a drop.

Families are going under because of a wheels-off approach to scheduling activities. And one of the best ways to keep that from happening is by using a "kid lid." Parents need to put kid lids on their children's schedules. Without that lid, that security measure, unnecessary activities can spill out and threaten to mess up the family.

My wife and I have installed a kid lid by adopting a one-to-one ratio. In other words, we allow each child to select one major activity per season. Sometimes they choose not to do any activity for a season, and that is okay; children don't have to participate in extracurricular opportunities 365 days a year. If each child gets involved in more than one activity at a time, your family is running the risk of experiencing some serious overcommitment, overstimulation, and over-the-top trouble. Your family will end up hydroplaning over life and living on the fly as opposed to being focused and intentional.

Schedule Downtime

In addition to using a kid lid, we also need to schedule downtime. It may seem paradoxical to say we need to *schedule* rest periods, but it's not. If you don't make room for it on your schedule, downtime won't happen. The Bible backs up this idea. In Psalm 46:10, God tells us, "Be still and know that I am God" (NIV). This indicates that there is a direct correlation between stillness and knowing God. So, we need to intentionally schedule those blank spots on our calendars.

What that means in practical terms is that we should have a night or two each week when nothing is on the agenda—no activity, program, game, concert, or church event. That might mean, if you can't get everyone's schedule to mesh, that some rehearsals and practices might need to be skipped in favor of family time. Ideally, you should try to schedule the activities in advance that allow for at least one open night a week as a family, but that may not always be feasible. So if push comes to shove, you may need to throw something from the schedule to open up this time.

This night should be for your family to just *chillax* (that means to chill out and relax) at home. And I'm not talking about watching television. Unplug from all of the technology that you have, and just unwind. You will be amazed at all of the creativity and innovation that will occur in your children's lives when they have the opportunity to relax. You will not believe how easily they will relate to you, and what comes out in conversations with one another, when you have downtime.

Right now, I would like to focus specifically on the educators who are reading this book. Downtime at home is just that—downtime. That does not include periods that the children spend in their rooms doing homework or studying. Now, I understand that there are certain bureaucratic pressures in educating our youth, but homework is not necessarily the answer. I remember, as a kid, spending hours upon hours locked away in my room, racking my brain to finish the homework I had been assigned. And what I remember most about those hours is not what I learned but how exhausted I was afterwards.

We need to work together as parents and teachers to reach a point that allows for both goals to be met—the goals of educating and parenting. Many teachers are realizing that the key to a good education doesn't lie in assigning hours of homework each night. A study published in *U.S. News & World Report* in October 2003 stated that only 33.4 percent of high school seniors in 2002 spent more than five hours a week on homework. That is wonderful news on the family front, because it allows the chance for more downtime at home. The article goes on to say that many schools are discovering that lower student-to-teacher ratios, rather than more homework, are a better stimulus toward increased educational achievement.[3]

In an interesting parallel, reports show that SAT test scores of the class of 2003 were at a sixteen-year high.[4] I'm not an educational expert or social scientist, but with the number of hours of homework down and SAT scores up, I might be tempted to conclude that more homework does not necessarily lead to a better education. As parents and educators alike, we must be open to the realization that too much homework is one factor hindering the growth of families and the ability to parent effectively.

Parents, downtime is good time. So make it happen! The benefits to your family, your marriage, and, might I add, to your emotional stability will be incredible. Kick back and let the creativity and conversation flow.

Don't Quit Your Job

In the next and final chapter, I'm going to show you how to work yourself out of a job as a parent. But I need to make sure you understand that I'm not contradicting myself as I give my final piece of advice for this chapter, which is one of the major tenets of the parent-CEO household and one that I have tried to reinforce throughout the book. And that is: *don't quit your job.*

I'm not referring to what you do professionally, or your job as a parent. I am referring to your number one responsibility in the family—that of being a spouse. I have addressed that from the very beginning. Too often, parents, when they crank out a couple of kids, step down from their main jobs of being husbands and wives. The husband steps down from being the husband. The wife steps down from her primary responsibility of being the wife. They immerse themselves in either their work, making the mean green, or orbiting their world around their children. Marital drift takes place, because there is no intimacy, no date night, no special time of communication. The kids run the show.

I see these couples all the time at church. When they come

to church, they can't even drop off their little ones at the nursery. The sound of the children's cries when they leave them is more than they can bear. So they bring their infants and toddlers into the auditorium, and they can't hear the message or experience God because they are distracting themselves and everyone around them. You may feel it's best to have your children with you in church, but I disagree. In my twenty years of experience in the ministry and as a father of four, I have found the best way for both children and adults to learn about God is through age-appropriate teaching. I do not understand churches that fail to provide a unique environment for children to learn and worship God in ways that are meaningful to them. This is part of the process of individuation. I challenge you to leave your children in the capable hands of the children's workers at your church so that you and others around you can enjoy the adult worship service. Forgive my tangent; I'll get off of my soapbox now.

So let's wake up, parents, and smell the Starbucks here. If you want to escape the Parent Zap, you must first commit yourself to your number one responsibility. It is not all about your kids. I love children, but it's time to put the family flow chart into action. It's about God first. Then it's about the second most important relationship behind God, your relationship with your spouse. And then, after that, your kids. Keeping the marriage relationship at the focal point of the home is the best thing you can do to keep your family priorities on track and on target.

You can go down the list: don't OD on options, use a kid lid, plan for downtime, and don't quit your job. Now that we have all this advice on how to schedule activities effectively in our lives, what do we do about it? How do we put this stuff into gear?

Society has its demands on our families. It tells us that in order to be a successful family, we need to overstimulate, over-commit, and OD on options. According to the world, if we do that, our family will be over the top. But the truth is the world's philosophy does not work. In Romans 12:2 God tells us, "Don't copy the behavior and customs of this world, but let God *transform* you into a new person by changing the way you think. Then you will know what God wants you to do, and you will know how good and pleasing and perfect his will really is."

The word *transform* in its original language is the basis for our word *metamorphosis*. God tells us that in order for our families to live according to his will, we are to go through a meta-morphosis. This means we have to be intentional about it and recognize that we cannot muster up the courage on our own to undergo this change. We simply cannot do it alone. As parents, we need to allow God to renew our minds as we focus on his agenda—"how good and pleasing and perfect his will really is."

I challenge you every day to look in the mirror and say, "God, show me how to live. Show me what I have to do to live out your priorities, to live out your agenda. I want to know what your perfect will and plan for my family is." Once we do that, we will discover how to maintain sanity in our schedule and escape the Parent Zap.

PART SIX

Conclusion

Embracing the
Ultimate Goal of
Parenting

{ 9 }

Working Yourself Out of a Job

LIFT WEIGHTS at a local health club three times a week, a routine I have maintained for many years. One day several years ago, I took my daughter LeeBeth with me to the weight room. We were having a great time hanging out in the gym together, and she watched as I went through my regular sets of squats, curls, and lifts, along with several other exercises. In the middle of my routine, I went over to the dumbbell rack to pull off another set and accidentally knocked a fifty-pound dumbbell off the rack and onto my toes.

I yelled in pain and crumpled to the floor. My big toe was broken in four places, and the bone was sticking out through the toenail. As if that weren't enough, my second toe was also broken. Fortunately, with the help of some great doctors, I was able to have my toes reconstructed and made usable again.

An interesting thing happened, though, as I was lying on the floor of that weight room, going into mild shock, with blood everywhere. LeeBeth, who was then only seven years old, was calm, cool, and collected. The adults around me were freaking out and saying comforting things like, "Ooh, aah, that looks awful, man." And "You might lose that toe. You know, I lost my toe one time; it was the worst thing in the world."

Meanwhile, LeeBeth calmly walked over to me and said, "Daddy, would you like for me to call Mommy?"

I said, "Yes, please."

She said, "Okay, I will." And she walked across the weight room to a pay phone and without hesitation dialed Lisa's number.

As I think back about how LeeBeth handled that situation almost ten years ago, I marvel at the unique individual she was then and has become today. And I can't help but celebrate the task of parenting, because that's one of the great things it's about. It's the parents' task to bring out the individuality in our children—to encourage and motivate and stimulate their God-given uniqueness. That is one of the biggest challenges I face, and if you are honest with yourself, it is one of the biggest challenges you face as well.

No other job is as rewarding, fulfilling, or difficult as that of being a parent. But just like our professional careers, parenting does have a beginning and an end. Some may say that once we have kids, we are parents for the rest of our lives. That is true, in a sense. But in very hands-on terms, it is a finite responsibility that ends when our kids leave home. After that, our relationship with our kids morphs into one of counselor and friend. We might even say that, as parents, we are actually working ourselves out of a job. And that is what we are going to address in this concluding chapter: how do we bring up our kids in such a way that we work ourselves out of a job?

It all begins by understanding, fully and completely, the goal of parenting we defined earlier. Once again, that goal is to teach and train our children to leave. We have seen that one of the biblical foundations for this parental benchmark is in Proverbs 22:6: "Train a child in the way he should go, / and when he is old he will not turn from it" (NIV). If we are to understand what it truly means to teach and train our children to leave home, we must first understand the original meaning behind this verse.

This verse from the Bible is often misquoted and misunderstood, and here is how most people interpret it: they say if you take children to church when they are young, if you teach them how to say prayers before meals, during emergency situations, or during difficult times, then as they get older—even though they sow the wild oats, go a little crazy—they will turn back to God and live happily ever after. But that interpretation does not hold biblical water.

I know many men and women whose parents took them to church every time the doors opened, but some of those children went wild, ran from God, and never returned. How can that be? How could they be brought up in such a religious environment and run away from God? Isn't this verse a promise that if their parents raised them to believe in God, they would turn out all right? I'm sorry to be the bearer of bad news, but this verse holds no such promise.

Please don't misunderstand me. I'm all for bringing kids to church on a regular basis—I think I've established quite clearly my feelings on that. But as awesome as that is to do, it does not promise a guaranteed outcome. You are sweetening the odds considerably, but there simply are no formulas for getting your kids to turn out a certain way. I wrote in the last chapter that it is your job to provide a disciplined home and that we can't blame our kids if discipline is lacking. While that's true, it does not mean that an exemplary home of loving and consistent discipline will produce an exemplary child. Your job is to run your family the best way you know how with God's help. The outcome, unfortunately, is out of your hands because children grow up with minds and hearts and wills of their own.

Rather, these words in Proverbs are words of challenge that tell us parents we should bring out the individuality and the unique qualities in our children. I will develop this idea further, but when we teach them the "way they should go," we are basically helping them find their own places in life according to the ways God has uniquely gifted them. That looks so elementary, so easy to do in print, but really making it happen in your family and mine is a difficult process.

Discern Their Uniqueness

I want to explore several challenges we face, parents, if we are going to go about the task of drawing out this individuality in our children. The first is that we must discern the uniqueness of our children. If I am really going to be a parent who draws this out, I have to learn to recognize the uniqueness of LeeBeth, EJ, Laurie, and Landra. How do I do that? How do you do that with your kids?

Let's jump right into Proverbs 22:6 and find out. We are going to take this verse, put it on the operating table, and dissect it. First of all, look at the phrase "train a child." Let's consider the word "child" first. This is not referring just to an infant. A child is any one of your offspring, parents, who lives under your roof. Any child, from three to twenty-three, who is still under your authority should be open to your training.

The word *train* is an interesting word that means "to know," because we can't train something unless we first know something. There are two beautiful pictures behind this Hebrew term. The first picture is that of training a horse. If you trained a wild horse back in biblical times, you put a rope in between its teeth to control it and calm it. This action prepared the horse to take direction from its master. It was a picture of submission. But the master had to build a relationship of trust with the horse, to know the horse, before it would submit to the control of the rope.

The second picture is one of a Hebrew midwife. After birth, she took her index finger, placed it in a little jar of fig juice, put the fig juice around the gums of the infant, started the sucking motion, and then gave the infant to the mom to breast-feed. She was awakening the child's sucking instincts so that he could begin to nourish himself from his mother's breast. This is a picture of giving a child direction, even as an infant, toward becoming self-sufficient. Thus, we are to bring our children into a place of submission, and at the same time, give them direction toward individuality. But we cannot do these things unless we are able to truly discern their uniqueness.

Let's think about this word *discern*. How do we really discern their uniqueness? As I mentioned earlier in the book, for years child development experts espoused the "lump of clay" theory. They said children are like lumps of clay, and you can mold them, shape them, and make them into anything you want them to be. Today, though, these same experts are confirming the truth of the Bible—that each individual is unique. Again, these experts were kidding us, because that theory is a joke. These lumps of clay have abilities, aptitudes, and little wills and minds of their own. They are completely different from anybody else on the planet.

Just think about your own children. One might have come into the world with a smile on his face and an olive branch in his teeth, the other with a smirk on his face and a cigar between his teeth. The differences from the very beginning are truly phenomenal, and it is our job as parents to draw out, to discern, those differences in our kids.

One year some friends and I went fishing in Port O'Connor, Texas. The guide we were with, Joe, was a wildlife expert, so we also engaged in a little wildlife observation. Every once in a while, he pointed out unique fish, plants, and birds. He regaled us with little-known facts about their characteristics, their habitats, their feeding habits. To be honest, we were blown away by how much this guy knew. And how did Joe the wildlife expert get such a wealth of knowledge? He was an expert in the field of wildlife because he had studied it for years. He sat back and observed it, day after day after day. And he took note of it all.

Parents, we need to take another kind of tour—a *childlife* tour—to observe our children and come to understand them in a real and intimate way. We may even need to write down their unique character qualities, feeding patterns, gifts, and aptitudes. Just because you conceived them, carried them, brought them into the world, put clothes on their backs and food on the table doesn't mean you know your children. It takes time, it takes observation, and it takes years of patience and understanding to discern your children's uniqueness. So begin now, strategically and intentionally, to get to know your kids so you can encourage their individuality.

Affirm Their Bents

Bent. That's a strange term, isn't it? Well, your children have certain bents that you as a parent need to affirm. And once again, we can go back to Proverbs 22:6 to find out what that means. We will be examining the second phrase of this sentence: "Train a child in *the way he should go.*" The word *way* in Hebrew, the original language of the Old Testament, actually means "bent." You will also find this term in Psalm 11:2, where it refers to the "bend" of a bow.

A bow has a certain bent to it. And during the time when this proverb was penned, when hunters made their own bows, they gave great care to the selection of a suitable piece of wood. They didn't just walk out to the first nice-looking tree, break off a limb, and make a bow out of it, thinking, "This will do. This limb will be okay for hunting and shooting wild game." They weren't that careless, because the bent of the limb was the key to making a great hunting instrument. They searched and searched and searched some more until finally they saw the perfect tree with the perfect limb with the perfect grain, growing properly with that natural bent already in place. They then cut that limb off and used it to make a bow.

So, you see, from the literal Hebrew, the first part of Proverbs 22:6 could be translated like this: "Train up a child according to his ways." Every child has a bent. Each has a talent, an ability that other children don't have. And parents, if we are going to affirm our kids' bents, we must first discern them.

In other words, we have to discover them and then find ways to bring them out.

How do you bring out that bent? You have to expose your children at a very, very early age to a number of challenges, opportunities, and avenues. And as you present these things to them, you watch and see what really puts wind in their sails, what really turns them on and fires up their engines. And when you discern that, you need to take note of it: "I think that might be his bent; that might be his thing. I should encourage this activity or skill or talent." Provide these opportunities, of course, keeping in mind the balance we addressed in the previous chapter.

When LeeBeth was seven, the same year I broke my big toe, I remember asking her this question: "LeeBeth, what do you like to do more than anything in the world?"

She replied, "I like to draw, and I like to paint."

I asked, "LeeBeth, how do you feel about painting? How do you really feel when you are drawing?"

I'll never forget what she said to me. "Daddy, I feel proud of myself." *Ding, ding, ding, ding. We have a winner!* The bells and whistles sounded in my brain, because that was most likely one of LeeBeth's natural bents. I am an amateur artist, and I could sense in her the same passions I've had for drawing and painting. God chose to take my life in a different direction professionally, but that inclination is still there.

Over the years, I've continued to observe LeeBeth and give her avenues that affirm her bent because of what I observed several years ago. She is now a teenager and can choose to take her life in a number of different directions, but I believe this particular gift will always be a part of what she does because we, as her parents, discerned it and have affirmed it.

If your children are already older and you feel you've missed out on affirming their bents early on, don't despair. You will see those gifts, talents, and abilities become evident throughout childhood and the teen years. You can recognize and affirm these at any age through your day-to-day contact with your kids. Wherever your children are along this journey, begin to affirm their uniqueness now.

One practical way we can affirm our kids' natural bents is with words. When was the last time you told your son or daughter, "You are special" or "I noticed how well you did that"? Brag on them. Brag on the gifts and talents you see in them. It will revolutionize your child's outlook on life if you look him or her in the eye and say, "You know what? You are so unique, and your personality is so special. You see, God wired you up the way he did for a reason and wants you to be a one-of-a-kind individual." When children understand that trajectory-changing statement, when they own the fact that they are unique, they will be propelled with full velocity into a life of meaning and purpose. They will be able to take their particular bents and use them like bows and arrows to hit a bull's-eye with their lives.

Parents, though, can make some crucial mistakes as they look at their children's abilities and try to affirm their "bentness." Let's look at some of these problems.

Don't Play the Comparison Game

First of all, it is unfair to compare your children with other children, even in your own family. Don't play that game. Are you familiar with the biblical story of Joseph? Joseph's father was the quintessential comparer when it came to his sons. He made it very clear to everyone, his family included, that

Joseph was his favorite. And it ended up tearing the family apart. Because of their jealousy, Joseph's brothers conspired against him, threw him into a pit, and had him sold into slavery. This father lost his son, until they were reunited many years later, simply because he dared to compare him with the rest of his children.

Or how about the biblical lesson from the lives of a husband and wife named Isaac and Rebecca? I can really identify with this couple because they had twins, Esau and Jacob. Esau was an outdoorsman. If he were living today, he would read magazines like *Sports Afield* and watch fly-fishing shows on the Outdoor Channel. Esau went hunting almost every day and took his four-wheel-drive chariot out on the weekends for little off-road excursions. You know the type. He was a man's man, so to speak. And his father loved him. It was only natural for Isaac to pat his son on the behind and say, "You are *it*, son. You're just like your old man, a chip off the old block." I can imagine them wrestling with each other and punching each other on the arm now and then. This father and son were tight.

But the other son, Jacob, was a little different. You see, Isaac didn't relate very well to Esau's twin brother. Jacob liked to cook, hang out in the kitchen, and do things that didn't jibe with his father's particular interests. Today, Jacob might have been an art and music lover, a creative type with soft hands and a tender heart. Think about how men like that are stereotyped today, and then imagine what it must have been like for Jacob thousands of years ago, in that very patriarchal time period. This comparison game helped create a rift between Jacob and Esau that is still evident in the Middle East tensions in our world today.

Do you see, parents, how unfair it is to compare? And not only is it unfair, it is potentially devastating to the well-being of your kids and your entire family.

Don't Force It

Parents also make another critical mistake. Oftentimes, they can knock their children off course by forcing them to do things the parents want for them instead of the things the kids want for themselves. It's as if you put some space-age parental force field around your child, pushing her toward certain interests and barring her from other interests.

Now, I'm not referring to activities or interests that are harmful or morally wrong; that's another issue entirely. What I'm referring to is an attempt, similar to what I mentioned in the previous chapter, by parents to remake their kids in their own image or into some fantasy image they always wished for themselves but could never fulfill.

A good example of this is what I did when I discovered the artistic ability in LeeBeth. I could have gone full tilt over that. I could have had her scheduled in every art class under the sun, sat with her every day to make sure she honed her skills, and as she got older dogged her about attending an art school. But fortunately, I kept a cool head and didn't push her about this. I encouraged her. I affirmed her. But I didn't force the issue. I knew that, if this was something that was meant to be, it would have to be her choice.

Sadly, though, cooler heads do not prevail on athletic fields, platforms, and recital halls across the country. I see a bunch of freaked-out fathers and mesmerized mothers everywhere I go. Attend a Little League soccer game sometime, and watch the reactions of the parents toward these little five- and six-year-olds. Go to a beauty pageant, ballet performance, or piano recital, and watch the determined faces of the grownups. Dads and moms are losing it when it comes to the critical issue, by piling pounds of pressure on the fragile frames of their children.

Parents, please maintain a balance in this area. Yes, affirm, love, support, and encourage. But at the end of the day, realize it is only God's amazing grace and your child's own determination that will decide what your child does or does not do in life. Provide your children with tools and opportunities, celebrate their giftedness, coach them when needed, affirm their bents, and then step back and let God take care of the rest.

Learn Their Languages

Here is my third and final challenge to you as you try to affirm the natural bents of your kids (and I have to admit that this is a tough one): we must learn the languages of our children. To illustrate this point, I need to take you back several years to a trip that Lisa and I took to Korea. We had a fabulous experience and developed a taste for Korean food that we still enjoy today. As we traveled through the countryside, speaking and doing mission work in various places, we got to see parts of Korea that most people don't—the back roads, the public schools, the home life of the locals, the little churches and small roadside businesses.

A few times during our stay, I attempted conversation with the Korean faculty and students at the school where we were working. But guess what? We were unable to communicate. Since I didn't speak Korean and they didn't speak English, I reached a point of frustration and had to resign myself to conversing through an interpreter. I really wanted to talk to them in their own language, but I couldn't do it. They just looked at me, nodding and smiling, with kind of a blank look in their eyes. I even tried the typical thing that Americans do when someone doesn't understand what they are saying: I tried speaking louder. That didn't work either.

What does my experience in Korea have to do with learning the languages of our kids? Each of your children—whether you have one, two, three, four kids like me, six, or an even dozen—speaks a specific language. And you must learn those languages before you can effectively communicate with them. They want and need to receive communication from you that says, "I understand you and I'm going to approach you in the way you need to be approached." I'm referring not to their spoken language but to their "love language."

Gary Chapman has written several books on the subject of love languages that I highly recommend as you seek to improve communication with your kids.[1] One of the ways, Chapman says, that some children express and receive love is through physical touch. They like to get a bear hug from Mommy or Daddy, to get a little squeeze on the shoulder, or a pat on the back. These kids express and receive love through these physical expressions. My son EJ is a hugger, and we've learned that he responds well to physical affirmation.

Other kids like verbal expressions of love. Hearing that Mommy and Daddy love them is more meaningful than getting a hug. They like hearing, "You are special. I love you just the way you are." Or they might even express their love in writing or like to receive expressions of love in writing from others. My twins, in particular, like to write little notes of love to me wherever and whenever they get the chance: on scraps of paper, on notepads, on chalkboards, dry-erase boards, and on napkins.

Chapman says that other kids express love by giving. The gifts they give and receive are very meaningful. My father is a giver. He sometimes hands us a couple of airline tickets, saying, "Ed, take Lisa and go to this exotic location." And I know it's Dad's way of communicating his love to us.

LeeBeth is sixteen now, and in addition to appreciating physical affirmation, she likes to give and receive gifts. (My personal belief is that all kids move automatically into the love language of receiving gifts the minute they turn thirteen. You know I'm joking, but teens do like to get stuff, don't they?)

Time is another of the love languages. You can communicate love by just hanging out with your kids. Your child may really respond to times when you are able just to relax together and kick back. Are you giving that quality time to your children? Time is one of our most precious commodities and can be one of our most precious expressions of love.

Are you tuning in to the special languages of your children? If not, you could be pushing them to find that love and affirmation somewhere else. For example, let's say a certain dad has a teenage daughter whose language of love is hugging. She needs that physical affirmation from him, but Dad doesn't hug his daughter much. When she gets to be thirteen or older, she will begin to really long for that physical affirmation and will end up falling into the arms of the first guy who winks and whistles at her. And the kind of touching he'll be doing will not be respectful, nonsexual touching. What a sad, sad scenario.

Don't let something like that happen in your family. Learn your kids' languages, and take the time and effort to communicate to them in ways that are especially meaningful for them.

*   *   *

Mom and Dad, are you paying attention to the beauty of the bow? Have you mastered the secret of the "bent"? When you apply these three principles of uniqueness in the lives of your children, you will be ready to let your children go. You will be prepared to release the arrow of your child's life into the world, because you know it will go straight toward the target and hit the bull's-eye every time. My prayer for you, parents, as well as for Lisa and myself, is that we will be about the business of becoming parents who know how to shoot those unique arrows toward the target for the glory of God.

When it comes right down to it, parenting is a celebration of the uniqueness and individuality of children. And when your kids do finally leave home, you will be rejoicing, not because you're glad to see them go, but because you have done what God wanted you to do. That's what it's all about—coming to the end of the adolescent road and seeing your children blossom into loving, caring adults with all of the character qualities, skills, and confidence they need to make it on their own. Are your kids preparing for that? Are you? At the end of the day, will you be able to say, "We've done our job, son. We've done our job, daughter. We are ready to let you go"?

That's the end of the parenting road, but it all begins with a commitment to become a parent CEO. Have you made that commitment? Allowing your children to turn into kid CEOs and run your life is not good for them or good for you. If you want them to face the road of life with self-assurance, follow God's dynamic design for the family: God, marriage, kids. It will bring order to your home, vibrancy to your marriage, security to your family, and sanity to your life.

Notes

Introduction

1. U.S. Census 2000, "America's Families and Living Arrangements," http://www.census.gov/prod/2001pubs/p20–537.pdf, 7.

Chapter 1

1. George Barna, *Transforming Your Children into Spiritual Champions* (Ventura, CA: Regal Books, 2003), 23.

2. Dr. James Dobson, *The New Dare to Discipline* (Wheaton, IL: Tyndale House Publishers, 1992), 60.

3. Jim Collins, *Good to Great* (New York: HarperCollins Publishers, 2001), 41–42.

4. Gary Smalley, *The Key to Your Child's Heart* (Dallas, TX: Word Publishing, 1992), 55.

5. Stuart Shepard, "Experts Say Kids Need More Sleep," Family News in Focus, April 28, 2003, http://family.org/cforum/fnif/news/a0025701.cfm.

6. Gary Chapman, *Covenant Marriage* (Nashville, TN: Broadman & Holman Publishers, 2003), 99.

7. Dr. Henry Cloud and Dr. John Townsend, *Boundaries in Marriage* (Grand Rapids, MI: Zondervan Publishing House, 1999), 147.

8. Laura L. Smith, Ph.D., and Charles H. Elliott, Ph.D., *Hollow Kids* (Roseville, CA: Prima Publishing, 2001), 220.

Chapter 2

1. John Rosemond, *Six-Point Plan for Raising Happy, Healthy Children* (Kansas City, KS: Universal Press Syndicate Company, 1989), 6.

2. Carol Lynn Mithers, "The Perils of the Pushover Parent," *Ladies' Home Journal*, January 2003, 92.

3. Dr. Henry Cloud and Dr. John Townsend, *Boundaries with Kids* (Grand Rapids, MI: Zondervan Publishing House, 1998), 45.

4. Gary Smalley as quoted by Gloria Gaither, in *What My Parents Did Right* (West Monroe, LA: Howard Publishing Company, 2002), 230.

5. Dr. Henry Cloud and Dr. John Townsend, *Boundaries in Marriage,* 149.

Chapter 3

1. Dr. James Dobson, *Bringing Up Boys* (Wheaton, IL: Tyndale House Publishers, 2001), 206.

2. Dr. Henry Cloud and Dr. John Townsend, "Children with Boundaries and the Parents Who Taught Them," Family.org, http://www.family.org/pplace/schoolkid/a0006045.cfm. Adapted from *Boundaries with Kids* (Grand Rapids, MI: Zondervan, 1998).

3. Kurt and Olivia Bruner, "Parenting on Purpose," Family.org, http://www.family.org/pplace/newparent/a0021344.cfm. Adapted from *The Family Compass* (Colorado Springs: Chariot Victor Publishing).

4. Lisa Beamer, "Staying Focused on Godly Values," Suite101.com, October 1, 2000, http://www.suite101.com/article.cfm/christian_families/49303.

5. I first heard this term from psychologist and author Dr. Henry Cloud.

6. John Rosemond, *Six-Point Plan for Raising Happy, Healthy Children,* 3.

7. Ricky Byrdsong, "Coaching Your Kids in the Game of Life—Part 2," www.family.org, http://www.family.org/pplace/newparent/a0023501.cfm. Adapted from *Coaching Your Kids in the Game of Life* (Bloomington, MN: Bethany House Publishers, 2000).

Chapter 4

1. "MTV, at 20, Rocks on Its Own," *USA Today,* August 1, 2001, http://www.usatoday.com/life/television/2001-08-01-mtv-at-20.htm.

2. Dr. James Dobson, *Bringing Up Boys,* 203–204.

3. "In a Nation Aflutter," *USA Today,* February 3, 2004.

4. "TV's Frisky Family Values," *U.S. News & World Report,* April 15, 1996.

5. "Meanness Sells, But For How Long?" *USA Today,* August 25, 2003.

6. Ibid.

7. "Family TV Goes Down the Tubes," *Newsweek,* February 23, 2003, http://www.msnbc.msn.com/id/4271882.

8. Http://www.screenit.com. Screenit.com is a free online movie review service for families.

9. Http://www.previewonline.org. Previewonline.org is a subscription-based online and print Christian movie and TV review service but allows free access to mini reviews on their Web site.

10. "Pornography Statistics 2003," Internet Filter Review, http://www.internetfilterreview.com/internet-pornography-statistics.html.

11. Ibid.

12. Pamela Dillon, "Internet Safety: Protect Your Children from the Internet's Seamy Side," http://childrentoday.com/resources/articles/internetsafety.htm.

13. Larry Copeland, "Seventy-Seven Percent Back Ten Commandments," *USA Today,* August 28, 2003.

14. "More Companies Downsize Family-friendly Programs," *USA Today,* October 20, 2003.

15. William Kilpatrick, *Why Johnny Can't Tell Right from Wrong* (New York: Simon and Schuster, 1992), 19–20.

16. Ibid.

17. Ibid., 74.

18. "Family TV Goes Down the Tube," *Newsweek.*

19. George Barna, *Transforming Your Children into Spiritual Champions,* 23.

20. "Who's in Charge Here?" *Time,* August 6, 2001.

21. William Kilpatrick, 28.

22. Ibid., 268–315.

Chapter 5

1. Noel Horner, "Society's Slide into Sexual Immorality," United Church of God St. Paul, 1997, http://www.ucgstp.org//lit/gn/gn010/immoral.html.

2. Edward J. Barks, "How Important Are Nonverbal Signals?," November 2003, http://www.barkscomm.com/personaltrainer/PT00060.asp.

Chapter 6

1. Gary Chapman, *Covenant Marriage,* 181.

2. Willard F. Harley Jr., *Give and Take: The Secret to Marital Compatibility* (Grand Rapids, MI: Fleming H. Revell, 1996), 188–190. I modified this illustration slightly from the way Harley writes it in his book.

3. Robert and Rosemary Barnes, *Great Sexpectations* (Grand Rapids, MI: Zondervan Publishing House, 1996), 27.

4. Ibid., 106.

5. Gary Chapman, *Covenant Marriage*, 192–193.

6. Ibid., 39.

7. Jerry B. Jenkins, *Loving Your Marriage Enough to Protect It* (Chicago: Moody Press, 1993), 89.

Chapter 7

1. Proverbs 1:7.

2. Proverbs 29:15.

3. Proverbs 29:17.

4. The preceding paragraphs on single parents and the blended family, especially as it relates to discipline in the home, were adapted from my book *The Creative Marriage* (Grapevine, TX: Fellowship Resources, 2002), 132–134.

5. Dr. James Dobson, *The New Dare to Discipline*, 22.

6. John Rosemond, *Six-Point Plan for Raising Happy, Healthy Children*, 49.

7. George Barna, *Transforming Your Children into Spiritual Champions*, 21.

8. Dr. Henry Cloud and Dr. John Townsend, *Boundaries with Kids*, 208.

9. Gary Smalley, *The Key to Your Child's Heart*, 54.

10. David and Claudia Arp, *Answering the 8 Cries of the Spirited Child* (West Monroe, LA: Howard Publishing Company, 2003), 104.

11. Ed Young, *Against All Odds* (Nashville, TN: Thomas Nelson Publishers, 1992), 65.

12. Jessica Reaves, "Survey Gives Children Something to Cry About," *Time*, October 5, 2000, http://www.time.com/time/education/article/0,8599,56808,00.html.

13. Ibid.

14. Onita Nakra, "Dealing with a strong-willed child," *Gulf News*, February 14, 2003, http://www.gulfnews.com/Articles/people-places.asp?ArticleID=77379.

15. James Dobson, "The Strong-Willed Child: 12 Concepts and Ideas That May Be Helpful," http://www.new-life.net/parent02.htm. Adapted from *The Strong-Willed Child* (Wheaton, IL: Tyndale Publishers, 1992).

16. Ibid.

17. Gary Smalley, *The Key to Your Child's Heart*, 57.

Chapter 8

1. Barbara Kantrowitz and Pat Wingert, "The Parent Trap," *Newsweek,* January 29, 2001, 48.

2. Ed Young, *High Definition Living* (West Monroe, LA: Howard Publishing, 2003), 202.

3. Ulrich Boser, "Overworked and underplayed?" *U.S. News & World Report,* October 13, 2003, 51.

4. "SAT Scores Show 'Right Direction,'" August 26, 2003, http://www.councilofcollaboratives.org/files/satscoresshow082703.doc.

Chapter 9

1. I recommend the following titles by Gary Chapman on the subject of love languages: *The Five Love Languages, The Five Love Languages for Children,* and *The Five Love Languages for Teenagers.*

About the Author

Ed Young is the founding and senior pastor of Fellowship Church, one of the top ten fastest-growing churches of the past century. Ed is also seen and heard nationally on his syndicated daily radio broadcast and weekly television program *Creative Connection,* seen on TBN and Daystar. Ed is the author of *High Definition Living: Bringing Clarity to Your Life's Mission, Know Fear: Facing Life's Six Most Common Phobias,* and *Fatal Distractions: Overcoming Obstacles that Mess Up Our Lives.* He is coauthor of two books: *The Creative Marriage* (with Lisa Young) and *Can We Do That? 24 Innovative Practices That Will Change the Way You Do Church* (with Andy Stanley). He and his wife, Lisa, have four children.

To learn more about Ed Young's television or radio broadcasts, or for information about his other books and resources, visit www.creativecon-nection.org or www.fellowshipchurch.com or write him at:

Creative Connection with Ed Young
P.O. Box 619005
Dallas, TX 75261-9005
1-888-804-1999

More from Warner Faith

Coaching Your Kids to Be Leaders

Pat Williams

As senior executive vice president of the Orlando Magic and former general manager of the Philadelphia 76ers, Pat Williams knows how to nurture young talent and instill the passion, commitment, and determination necessary to become a champion. In this essential guide for parents, coaches, teachers, and all adults who work with and care about young people, Williams distills his wisdom into six key principles of leadership—Vision, Communication, People Skills, Character, Boldness, and Servanthood—and shows adults how to motivate and inspire children to avoid common pitfalls and negative peer pressure so they can become leaders in every area of their lives, both present and future. This insightful book features numerous personal success stories from many well-known leaders, including General Richard Meyers, chairman of the Joint Chiefs of Staff; Jeb Bush, governor of Florida; John Wooden, former UCLA coach; Edward Malloy, president of Notre Dame; and Mark Foley, U.S. congressman. *Coaching Your Kids to Be Leaders* will be an invaluable tool for those committed to building leadership skills in the children they care for.

COMING JANUARY 2005